AIR FRYER COOKBOOK FOR ONE:

The Complete Beginners Guide to 100+ Yummy, Affordable & Super-Easy Air Fryer Recipes for Weight Loss and Healthy Living

BONNIE C. PERRY

Table of Contents

BOOK DESCRIPTION 5

INTRODUCTION 6
- What is Air Fryer? 6
- How Does Your Air Fryer Function? 7
- Advantages of Using an Air Fryer 7
- Cooking Techniques for the Air Fryer 9
- Important Things to Remember 9
- Which Air Fryer is the Best for Me? 10
- Cleaning and Maintaining an Air Fryer 11

CHAPTER 1: BREAKFAST RECIPES 13
1. Vegetable Egg Soufflé 13
2. Chocolate-Filled Doughnut Holes 14
3. Mixed Berry Muffins 14
4. Strawberry Toast 16
5. Tender Monkey Bread with Cinnamon 17
6. Cheesy Hash Brown 18
7. Tex-Mex Hash Browns 18
8. Puffed Egg Tarts 19
9. Air Fryer Bacon 20
10. Breakfast Frittata 21
11. Morning Mini Cheeseburger Sliders 21
12. Avocado and Blueberry Muffins 22
13. Cheese Omelette 23
14. Cauliflower Rice Bowls 24
15. Red Cabbage Bowls 24
16. Mixed Veggie Bake 25
17. Cinnamon Pudding 25
18. Paprika Broccoli and Eggs 26
19. Zucchini Fritters 27
20. Broccoli Cheese Quiche 27
21. Bacon and Egg Bite Cups 28
22. Air Fryer Sausage 29
23. Bacon Grilled Cheese 29

CHAPTER 2: LUNCH RECIPES 31
24. Crusted Chicken Drumsticks 31
25. Lemony Salmon 32
26. BBQ Turkey Meatballs with Cranberry Sauce 33
27. Beef & Veggie Spring Rolls 34
28. Lemon Garlic Shrimp 35
29. Parsley Catfish 36
30. Easy Italian Meatballs 37
31. Crispy Haddock 38
32. Fennel and Tomato Stew 39
33. Spinach and Olives 39
34. Turkey and Broccoli Stew 40
35. Zucchini Stew 40
36. Pork Stew 41

37.	Chicken and Celery Stew	42
38.	Okra and Green Beans Stew	42
39.	Chimichurri Skirt Steak	43
40.	Air Fryer Buffalo Mushroom Poppers	44
41.	Cabbage and Radishes Mix	45
42.	Charred Bell Peppers	46
43.	Garlic Tomatoes	46
44.	Cauliflower Fritters	47
45.	Spiced Nuts	48
46.	Garlic Cauliflower Tots	49
47.	Coriander Artichokes	50
48.	Spinach and Artichokes Sauté	50

CHAPTER 3: DINNER RECIPES 52

49.	Parmesan Shrimp	52
50.	Tuna Chipotle	53
51.	Spicy Duck Legs	53
52.	Thai Sweet Chili Garlic Shrimp	54
53.	Lemon Chili Prawns	55
54.	Lemony and Spicy Coconut Crusted Salmon	56
55.	Green Onions & Parmesan Tomatoes	57
56.	Green Bell Peppers with Cauliflower Stuffing	58
57.	Cheesy Chickpea & Courgetti Burgers	59
58.	Spicy Sweet Potatoes	59
59.	Rice in Crab Shell	60
60.	Crab Fingers	61
61.	Saba Fish	62
62.	African Tilapia	63
63.	Chili Sea Bass	64
64.	Marinated Cod	64
65.	Glazed Pork Shoulder	65
66.	Pork Shoulder with Pineapple Sauce	66
67.	Air Fryer Ranch Pork Chops	67
68.	Rib-Eye Steak	68
69.	Breaded Air Fryer Pork Chops	69
70.	Glazed Pork Shoulder	70
71.	Pork Shoulder with Pineapple Sauce	70
72.	Rib-Eye Steak	72
73.	Breaded Air Fryer Pork Chops	73
74.	Flank Steak Beef	73
75.	Pepper Pork Chops	74
76.	Garlic Butter Pork Chops	75
77.	Five Spice Pork	75
78.	Roasted Lamb	76
79.	Juicy Pork Chops	77

CHAPTER 4: SNACKS AND DESSERTS 79

80.	Sugary Apple Fritters	79
81.	Baked Bacon Potatoes	80
82.	Raspberry Cream Roll-Ups	81
83.	Apricots in Blankets	82
84.	Radish Chips	83
85.	Air Fried Corn	84
86.	Avocado and Raspberries Cake	84
87.	Walnut and Vanilla Bars	85
88.	Plum Cream	85

89.	Mini Lava Cakes	86
90.	Lemon Blackberries Cake	87
91.	Chocolate Mug Cake	87
92.	Dark Chocolate Cheesecake	88
93.	Cream Doughnuts	89
94.	Coconut Balls	90
95.	Jicama Fries	90
96.	Kale Chips	91
97.	Finger Cookies	91
98.	Spicy Air-Fryer Sunflower Seeds	92
99.	Roasted Jack-O'-Lantern Seeds with black pepper	93
100.	Tasty Ranch Roasted Almonds	93
101.	Air-Fryer Jalapeño Poppers	94
102.	Simple Baked Brie with Orange Marmalade and Spiced Walnuts	95
103.	Crusted Pickle Chips	96
104.	Spicy Cumin Chickpeas	96
105.	Apple Doughnuts	97

CONCLUSION 99

BOOK DESCRIPTION

Do you want to learn everything there is to know about the air fryer?

The air fryer cooks food by circling it with hot air. One of its main advantages is the variety of cooking functions. It can bake and roast food as well as fry it. This handy appliance not only bakes cookies, cakes, and brownies, but it also makes a delicious roast dinner. The air fryer uses little to no oil to cook food. Furthermore, you won't have to spend hours washing multiple pots, pans, baking trays, or bowls. Simply gather and prepare all of your ingredients. Place them in the air fryer. Cooking time and temperature should be adjusted according to the recipe. Wait until the appliance beeps before serving your meal. The air fryer comes with all of the necessary accessories. You don't need to buy a basket, baking tray, or anything else. Simply put, an air fryer is easy to use and clean!

This cookbook contains the best one-person air fryer recipes in the following categories: Breakfast, Lunch, Dinner Snacks, and Desserts.

One of the benefits of the air fryer low carb recipes in this cookbook is that the ingredients can be found in any grocery store. So there's no need to order anything online or visit a specialty store. An air fryer is a simple cooking appliance that anyone can use. Crisp, fry, roast, grill, reheat, bake, and dehydrate are the most common cooking functions. It has easy-to-use controls for temperature, cooking time, start/stop, and power. A reversible rack, air fryer basket, dehydrating rack, and other useful accessories are included with the air fryer. You can cook your favorite foods such as French fries, pizza, casseroles, tacos, cakes, cookies, and brownies using its various programs.

Click the "buy now button"

INTRODUCTION

What is Air Fryer?

The air fryer is a common kitchen appliance used for frying foods such as meat, pastries, and potato chips.
To create a crunchy, crispy surface, heated air is blown around the dish.
This also causes the Maillard reaction, a chemical reaction. The reaction between an amino acid and a reducing sugar when heated changes the color and flavor of food.
Because of their lower fat and calorie content, air-fried foods are marketed as a healthier alternative to deep-fried foods.
Food can be air-fried with as little as a tablespoon (15 mL) of oil and still taste and feel like it was deep-fried.
Air frying is becoming increasingly popular because it allows you to cook delicious meals quickly and evenly with little fat and little effort. Here are a few reasons why you should switch to air frying:
It takes the place of other cooking appliances. The air fryer can replace your oven, microwave, deep fryer, and dehydrator. You can quickly cook perfect dishes for every meal using one small device without sacrificing flavor.
It cooks faster than conventional methods. Hot air is circulated around the cooking chamber during air frying. This results in faster and more even cooking while using a fraction of the energy that your oven does. Most air fryers have a maximum temperature of 400°F, so you can make almost anything in an oven in an air fryer.
It requires very little to no cooking oil. The ability to cook beautifully with little to no cooking oil is a major selling point for air fryers. Whether you're on a diet or not, you'll likely appreciate the lower fat and calorie content. The air fryer makes this possible.
Cleaning up is quick. Any method of cooking will leave your cooker dirty, but the smaller cooking chamber and removable basket of your air fryer make thorough cleanup a breeze!

How Does Your Air Fryer Function?

It uses a heating element and a fan circulating above, similar to a conventional oven, to convert the moisture in the food and air of the fryer into a mist. You put your food in the basket and place it in the main component of the Air Fryer. The extra-hot chamber allows a dry heat to penetrate through the food from the outside in, leaving it fully cooked with a nice crispy outside - the same result as a deep-fat fryer but without the extra calories! Another advantage is that because everything is in one basket, it is simple to clean up after your food has been removed! Air fryers use significantly less oil than other methods, such as deep-fat fryers, and thus produce meals with significantly lower fat content. Not only that, but it makes your kitchen safer for your children, with less chance of them injuring themselves as they might around an oven or deep-fat fryer. It is out of reach when placed on the countertop, giving you peace of mind while your food cooks.

Advantages of Using an Air Fryer

There are numerous advantages to using air fryer cooking appliances. These advantages include:
Food is prepared with little to no oil:
This appliance's main advantage is that it cooks food with little to no oil, which has numerous health benefits. It's also a great option for people who want to lose weight or reduce their fat intake.
Cleaning is a fairly simple process:
The cooking parts of the air fryer are removable. Remove them all and place them in the dishwasher before cleaning. But keep in mind not to put the main unit in the dishwasher or immerse it in water. This will cause damage to your appliance. A damp cloth can be used to clean the main unit. Reassemble the unit once all of the parts have dried.
Rapid and secure:
The air fryer is a cutting-edge cooking device. It cooks faster than other appliances, including the stove and oven. It is safe to use, produces little steam or heat, and does not risk spilling oil like deep-fat fryers. Cooking time and temperature can be adjusted according to the recipe. You can adjust the time and temperature on the air fryer's control panel, which has pre-set and user-friendly buttons.
There is no need for a stove or oven:
An air fryer can perform a variety of cooking tasks. You don't need a stove or oven to bake or roast food anymore; this versatile appliance can also grill, fry, and dehydrate food.
Minimal mess: Using an air fryer makes our kitchen easier to clean because there is no splattering oil or multiple dirty pans or trays to wash. The air fryer basket is also easy to clean because it is virtually nonstick and dishwasher safe.
The ideal companion for those who are always on the go:
The air fryer is an excellent addition to any kitchen because it allows for simple cooking with minimal effort. Gather your ingredients and place them in the air fryer basket. Start cooking after adjusting the cooking time, temperature, and desired functions.

Large capacity: Because the air fryer has a large capacity, you can cook meals for the entire family. For Christmas, you can even roast an entire turkey!

Saving time and money:

An air fryer is ideal for cooking food quickly. It also saves you money; with an air fryer, you can make your favorite restaurant dishes or takeout meals at home for a fraction of the price. Furthermore, by using less oil and ensuring that your ingredients are freshly prepared, you will make these meals healthier.

Healthy

The main health benefit of an air fryer is that it uses significantly less oil than a deep fryer. A significant portion of the used oil drains away without being absorbed by the food. You consume fewer calories and fat as a result.

The convection method used in these fryers promotes the Maillard reaction, a chemical process that results in browning. This has the added benefit of improving the appearance of the food while also improving its flavor and containing less fat.

Crispier Food

One of the best features of air fryers is their ability to produce crispy food without the use of oil. They do this by enclosing food in a perforated basket or on a rack and surrounding it with extremely hot air from all sides using convection-style heating.

As a result, air fryers are ideal for making crispy chips, onion rings, fish fingers, and other types of traditional fried food.

An air fryer produces crispier results than a conventional convection oven because it can cover the entire surface of the meal and the frying basket allows any excess fat to drop away.

Secure

Because they are self-contained appliances and use little hot fat in the cooking process, air fryers are generally safer. Splashes and burns are much less of an issue.

Machines are also designed to turn off when the timer expires to prevent the food from burning.

More Versatile

Most dishes that are traditionally cooked in a deep fryer can be prepared just as well, if not better, in an air fryer. There are numerous recipes to try out. Surprisingly, baked goods, vegetables, and steaks all do well.

Avoid Spreading Heat and Odor

Air fryers retain heat, so they do not raise the temperature of your kitchen like conventional ovens. This feature is especially useful if you live in a small house or apartment.

There are no intense aromas from deep frying because of the small amount of oil required.

Easy to Use

Air fryers are generally easy to use and require little supervision while cooking. Simply place the food in the basket, set the timer and temperature, and leave the rest to the fryer.

There are several simple recipes available if you need some ideas. I find frying vegetables to be incredibly simple and satisfying; the roasting effect makes the vegetables taste delicious.

Fat reduction

As previously stated, an Air Fryer uses significantly less oil to cook foods, resulting in less fat and calories in the meals you prepare. Who could resist the same delicious meals you love but with fewer calories and fat? Using less oil also means consuming fewer saturated fats, which are linked to an increased risk of cardiovascular disease, making Air Frying a healthier option all around.

Quicker meals

Air fryers cook food faster than conventional ovens and can even reheat food! Most foods can be reheated in the Air Fryer in 5 to 8 minutes without drying out or becoming rubbery. Chicken breasts cook in 10 to 15 minutes at 195°C, while steak cooks in the same time at 205°C! Frozen chips cook in 15 to 20 minutes at 205°C, becoming crispy and delicious. Nothing in an Air Fryer takes long, making it the master of quick healthy meals.

More meal options

When you're in a hurry, you'll probably find the quickest thing to throw in the oven - I know I do! The best thing about an Air Fryer is that it can quickly cook frozen and fresh foods, giving you a variety of options when you're in a hurry. Burgers, pork chops, salmon, and other foods can be cooked quickly in an Air Fryer, as can vegetable crisps, giving you more meal and snack options!

Using less energy

An Air Fryer uses significantly less energy than a conventional oven, which means you can save up to 50% on your electricity bill while cooking the same meal! For example, cooking chips in a fan-assisted oven typically costs around 35.38p, but this is reduced by 58% to only 14.62p when using your Air Fryer! With the price of electricity as it is, using an Air Fryer is a great way to save money and use less electricity.

Sufficient capacity

Air fryers are generally large enough. Standard Air Fryer capacity is around 4L, which is enough to feed a family of four comfortably. It is critical that you select the appropriate size for your needs, and it is always best to size up to ensure that you have enough space for all of your portions.

Cooking Techniques for the Air Fryer

Make sure you locate the best location for your Air Fryer. Leave enough space for the exhaust vent and place it on a heat-resistant countertop.

Get the correct Air Fryer accessories. There are plenty of silicone pan liners, muffin tins, and racks available for your Air Fryer, so stock up! They will help you broaden your horizons in terms of what you can make and make cleaning up even easier!

Fill the bottom with a slice of bread. It may sound strange, but placing a piece of bread beneath your food (especially if the bread is slightly stale) will help to catch any moisture or grease that comes out of your food - such as bacon - and save you time cleaning up.

Remember to shake your food to get an all-over crispy finish.

Important Things to Remember

Always keep the grate in the basket. This allows hot air to circulate around the food, preventing it from sitting in extra oil.

Air fryers make a noise. When it's turned on, you can hear the fans rotating.

It is beneficial. Remove the basket and turn the food around every few minutes to ensure even browning. You are welcome to take the basket and inspect it. This can be done at any time during the cooking process. The machine automatically turns off when the basket is removed, so there is no need to turn it off.

To avoid a fault, ensure that the drawer is fully inserted. The air fryer will notify you by going silent.

You aren't used to how quickly food cooks! It's one of the best features of the air fryer. There's probably a table in the manual for your air fryer with frying times and temperatures for common foods.

When there is less food in the basket, the cook time is reduced; when there is more food, the cook time is increased. You may require a slightly lower temperature. Many air fryer recipes require lower temperatures than traditional recipes. Believe it, even if it seems unlikely. Because air fryers heat up quickly and circulate hot air, a slightly lower temperature will help prevent food from becoming excessively black or crispy on the outside while still ensuring that the inside is cooked through.

Which Air Fryer is the Best for Me?

There are so many different types of air fryers to choose from that it's easy to become overwhelmed. To narrow down your options, ask yourself the following questions:
How many people will I be feeding?
What will I do with it? (I recommend you read some of the ideas in this book before answering that one!)
How often will I use it in my cooking?
Can I use a similar baking dish, bowl, or tray? (Important if you want to bake cakes or cookies)
Where will I keep it? (Consider the size of the fryer; they come in a variety of shapes and sizes.)
The remainder of this section contains additional information to assist you in making your decision.
Price
There are numerous models available, with prices ranging from around £40 to over £200. The cheapest air fryers have limited capacity and are best for cooking for one or cooking from frozen foods.
Air Fryers in Baskets and Ovens
Air fryers are classified into two types: basket air fryer (available in a variety of shapes and sizes) with a drawer that slides out to access the basket Some of these basket air fryers include paddles that turn and rearrange the food for you. Convection oven air fryers are the second type (these look more like microwave ovens). Convection oven air fryers combine an air fryer and a small oven; some can cook multiple trays of food at once and can even accommodate a rotisserie device. These air fryer/oven combos work more like a traditional convection oven and can be quite messy. The recipes and advice in this book are for basket-style, drawer-style air fryers without paddles.
How advanced do you want to be?

Manual controls are available on some air fryers, while touch screens are available on others. Also, many come with preset programs, which you may not use if you prefer to calculate your own cooking times. If you want to go really high-tech, consider purchasing a fryer with Wi-Fi, which will allow you to download an app that you can program and set in advance. However, you will still need to be present to shake the basket on occasion, so there is little benefit unless you have an appliance with a paddle that does the rearranging for you.
Dimensions and Capacity
Basket capacity ranges from 1 to 7 litres, and larger models have baskets large enough to hold a small chicken - though cooking a whole chicken in an air fryer is not recommended. Air fryers are best used for small items that cook quickly. The size of your fryer and the amount of food you're cooking will influence the cooking time, but most fryer recipes cook in 10-30 minutes. Overloading your fryer causes the food to become chewy and unpleasant to eat. To get the most out of an air fryer, choose one that comes with a compatible bowl, tray, and baking tin. The recipes in this book assume that you have these ingredients on hand (See Air Fryer Accessories.)

Cleaning and Maintaining an Air Fryer

Proper care and maintenance of your Air Fryer is essential if you want it to last longer and continue to help you cook delicious meals.
To begin, remove the basket and wash it in warm water with dish soap. Remove the basket from the outer section before washing to ensure you get into all the nooks and crannies.
Next, wipe the interior of the Air Fryer with a damp soapy cloth or sponge - don't forget the heating element! Once it's clean, wipe it down with a damp clean cloth and then again with a dry cloth.
It may appear to be a lot, but it only takes five minutes, if that, and by performing regular maintenance on your Air Fryer, you will extend its life and reduce the likelihood of having to purchase a new one!
Cleaning an air fryer is a breeze. You should follow the following instructions to keep the appliance in good working order:
Steel wire brushes, metal utensils, and abrasive sponges can scratch the surface of the main unit. They should not be used to remove leftover food from the air fryer basket because they can damage the surface.
Don't put the main unit in the dishwasher because it will be irreparably damaged.
Unplug the main unit from the socket before cleaning. Do not submerge the device in water.
After each use, clean the air fryer. The air fryer's components are all removable. Allow the main unit to cool before cleaning, then remove the accessories with oven gloves or tongs.
Clean the interior and exterior of the main unit with a damp cloth or a non-abrasive sponge.
Soak the air fryer basket in warm soapy water overnight to remove the grease.
For thorough cleaning, use a soft scrub brush, dishwashing liquid, baking soda, and a clean cloth.
Unplug the appliance and let it cool for 30 minutes before deep cleaning. Remove the air fryer pan and basket and wash them with hot water and soap. If you see grease on these parts, soak them for 10 minutes in hot water. Scrub with a non-abrasive sponge after that.
Wipe the interior of the basket with a damp cloth after cleaning it with washing up liquid.
Wipe the appliance gently with a moist or damp cloth.

If there is stubborn residue on the basket, combine baking soda and water and scrub the grime away with a soft brush.
Return all parts to the main unit once they have dried.
Before the next use, reassemble the air fryer.

CHAPTER 1: BREAKFAST RECIPES

1. Vegetable Egg Soufflé

Preparation Time: 10 minutes

Cooking Time: 20 minutes

Servings: 1

Ingredients:

4 large eggs

1 tsp. onion powder

1 tsp. garlic powder

1 tsp. red pepper, crushed

1/2 cup broccoli florets, chopped

1/2 cup mushrooms, chopped

Directions:

1. Sprinkle four ramekins with cooking spray and set aside.

2. In a bowl, whisk eggs with onion powder, garlic powder, and red pepper.

3. Add mushrooms and broccoli and stir well.

4. Pour egg mixture into the prepared ramekins and place ramekins into the air fryer basket.

5. Cook at 350 F for 15 minutes. Make sure soufflé is cooked if soufflé is not cooked, then cook for 5 minutes more.

6. Serve and enjoy.

Nutrition:

Calories: 91 kcal

Fat: 5.1g

Carbs: 4.7g

Protein: 7.4g

2. Chocolate-Filled Doughnut Holes

Preparation Time: 10 minutes

Cooking Time: 30 minutes

Servings: 1

Ingredients:

1 can refrigerated biscuits

Cooking oil spray

48 semisweet chocolate chips

3 tbsp. melted unsalted butter

¼ cup confectioners' sugar

Directions:

1. Separate the biscuits and cut each biscuit into thirds for 24 pieces.

2. Then, slightly flatten each biscuit piece and add 2 chocolate chips at the center. Around the chocolate, wrap the dough and seal the edges well.

3. Insert the crisper plate into the basket and the basket into the unit. Preheat the unit by selecting air fry, setting the temperature to 330°F, and setting the time to 3 minutes. Select start/stop to begin.

4. Once the unit is preheated, spray the crisper plate with cooking oil. Brush each doughnut whole with a bit of the butter and place it into the basket. Select air fry set the temperature to 330°F, and set the time between 8 and 12 minutes. Select start/stop to begin.

5. The doughnuts are done when they are golden brown. When the cooking is complete, place the doughnut holes on a plate and dust with the confectioners' sugar. Serve warm.

Nutrition:

Calories: 393 kcal

Fat: 17g

Carbs: 55g

Protein: 5g

3. Mixed Berry Muffins

Preparation Time: 15 minutes

Cooking Time: 15 minutes

Servings: 1

Ingredients:

1⅓ cups plus 1 tbsp all-purpose flour, divided

¼ cup granulated sugar

2 tbsp. light brown sugar

2 tsp. baking powder

2 eggs

⅔ cup whole milk

⅓ cup safflower oil

1 cup mixed fresh berries

Directions:

1. Stir together in a medium bowl, 1⅓ cups of flour, the granulated sugar, brown sugar, and baking powder until mixed well.

2. In a small bowl, whisk the eggs, milk, and oil until combined. Pure the egg mixture into the dry ingredients and mix until they combine.

3. In another small bowl, pitch the mixed berries with the leftover 1 tbsp of flour until coated. Gently stir the berries into the batter.

4. Two times the 16 foil muffin cups to make 8 cups.

5. Insert the crisper plate into the basket and the basket into the unit. Preheat the unit by selecting BAKE, setting the temperature to 315°F, and setting the time to 3 minutes. Select START/STOP to start.

6. Once the unit is preheated, place 4 cups into the basket and fill each three-quarter full with the batter.

7. Select BAKE, set the temperature to 315°F, and set the time for 17 minutes. Select START/STOP to begin.

8. After about 12 minutes, check the muffins. If they spring back when lightly touched with your finger, they are done. If not, resume cooking. When the cooking is done, transfer the muffins to a wire rack to cool. With the remaining muffin cups and batter, repeat steps 6, 7, and 8. Let the muffins cool for 10 minutes before serving.

Nutrition:

Calories: 230 kcal

Fat: 11g

Carbs: 30g

Protein: 4g

4. Strawberry Toast

Preparation Time: 8 minutes

Cooking Time: 10 minutes

Servings: 1

Ingredients:

4 slices bread, ½-inch thick

1 cup sliced strawberries

1 tsp. sugar

Cooking spray

Direction:

1. On a plate, place the bread slices.

2. Arrange the bread slices (sprayed side down) in the air fryer basket. Evenly spread the strawberries onto them and sprinkle them with sugar.

3. Put the air fryer lid on and cook in the preheated air fryer at 375°F for 8 minutes or until the tops are covered with a beautiful glaze.

4. Remove from the basket and serve on a plate.

Nutrition:

Calories: 375 kcal

Fat: 22g

Carbs: 2g

Fiber: 4g

Protein: 14g

5. Tender Monkey Bread with Cinnamon

Preparation Time: 5 minutes

Cooking Time: 10 minutes

Servings: 1

Ingredients:

1 can refrigerated biscuits

3 tbsp. brown sugar

¼ cup white sugar

½ tsp. cinnamon

⅛ tsp. nutmeg

3 tbsp. unsalted butter, melted

Direction:

1. On your cutting board, divide each biscuit into quarters.

2. Add the brown and white sugar, nutmeg, cinnamon to a mixing bowl and stir well.

3. Pour the melted butter into a medium bowl. Dip each biscuit in the melted butter, then in the sugar mixture to coat thoroughly.

4. Arrange the coated biscuits in a 6×6×2-inch baking pan and place the container into the air fryer basket.

5. Put the air fryer lid on and bake in batches in the preheated air fryer at 350°F for 6 to 9 minutes until set.

6. Then transfer it to a serving dish and cool for 5 minutes before serving.

Nutrition:

Calories: 1228 kcal

Fat: 42.64g

Carbs: 31.53g

Fiber: 1.2g

Protein: 49.97g

6. Cheesy Hash Brown

Preparation Time: 30 minutes

Cooking Time: 7-10 minutes

Servings: 1

Ingredients:

1½ lbs. hash browns

6 bacon slices, chopped.

8 oz. cream cheese, softened

1 yellow onion, chopped.

6 eggs

6 spring onions, chopped.

1 cup cheddar cheese, shredded

1 cup almond milk

A drizzle of olive oil

Salt and black pepper

Directions:

1. Heat your air fryer with the oil at 350°F. In a bowl, mix all other ingredients except the spring onions and whisk well.

2. Add this mixture to your air fryer, cover, and cook for 20 minutes.

3. Divide between plates, sprinkle the spring onions on top, and serve.

Nutrition:

Fat: 3.5g

Protein: 8g

Cholesterol: 20mg

Carbohydrate: 16g

Fiber: 1g

7. Tex-Mex Hash Browns

Preparation Time: 15 minutes

Cooking Time: 30 minutes

Servings: 1

Ingredients:

1½ pounds potatoes, peeled, cut into 1-inch cubes and soaked

1 red bell pepper, seeded and cut into 1-inch pieces

1 small onion, cut into 1-inch pieces

1 jalapeno, seeded and cut into 1-inch rings

1 tablespoon olive oil

½ teaspoon taco seasoning mix

½ teaspoon ground cumin

1 pinch salt and ground black pepper, to taste

Directions:

Preheat the Air fryer to 330 o F and grease an Air fryer basket.

Coat the potatoes with olive oil and transfer into the Air fryer basket.

Cook for about 18 minutes and dish out in a bowl.

Mix together bell pepper, onion, and jalapeno in the bowl and season with taco seasoning mix, cumin, salt and black pepper.

Toss to coat well and combine with the potatoes.

Transfer the seasoned vegetables into the Air fryer basket and cook for about 12 minutes, stirring in between.

Dish out and serve immediately.

Nutrition: Calories: 186, Fat: 4.3g, Carbohydrates: 33.7g, Sugar: 3g, Protein: 4g, Sodium: 79mg

8. Puffed Egg Tarts

Preparation Time: 10 minutes

Cooking Time: 42 minutes

Servings: 1

Ingredients:

1 sheet frozen puff pastry half, thawed and cut into 4 squares

¾ cup Monterey Jack cheese, shredded and divided

4 large eggs

1 tablespoon fresh parsley, minced

1 tablespoon olive oil

Directions:

Preheat the Air fryer to 390 °F

Place 2 pastry squares in the air fryer basket and cook for about 10 minutes.

Remove Air fryer basket from the Air fryer and press each square gently with a metal tablespoon to form an indentation.

Place 3 tablespoons of cheese in each hole and top with 1 egg each.

Return Air fryer basket to Air fryer and cook for about 11 minutes.

Remove tarts from the Air fryer basket and sprinkle with half the parsley.

Repeat with remaining pastry squares, cheese and eggs.

Dish out and serve warm.

Nutrition: Calories: 246, Fat: 19.4g, Carbohydrates: 5.9g, Sugar: 0.6g, Protein: 12.4g, Sodium: 213mg

9. Air Fryer Bacon

Preparation Time: 1 minutes

Cooking Time: 9 minutes

Servings: 1

Ingredients:

6 bacon strips

½ tablespoon olive oil

Directions:

Preheat the Air fryer to 350 °F and grease an Air fryer basket with olive oil.

Cook for about 9 minutes and flip the bacon.

Cook for 3 more minutes until crispy and serve warm.

Nutrition: Calories: 245, Fat: 17.1g, Carbohydrates: 10.2g, Sugar: 2.7g, Protein: 12.8g, Sodium: 580mg

10. Breakfast Frittata

Preparation Time: 10 minutes

Cooking Time: 15 minutes

Servings: 1

Ingredients:

6 eggs

8 cherry tomatoes, halved

2 tbsp. parmesan cheese, shredded

1 Italian sausage, diced

Salt and pepper, to taste

Directions:

Preheat your air fryer to 355°F. Add the tomatoes and sausage to the baking dish.

Place the baking dish into the air fryer and cook for 5 minutes.

Meanwhile, add eggs, salt, pepper, cheese, and oil into a mixing bowl, and whisk well.

Remove the baking dish from the air fryer and pour the egg mixture on top, spreading evenly.

Place the dish back into the air fryer and bake for additional 5 minutes.

Remove from the air fryer and slice into wedges and serve.

Nutrition: Calories: 273, Total Fat: 8.2 g, Carbs: 7 g, Protein: 14.2 g

11. Morning Mini Cheeseburger Sliders

Preparation Time: 10 minutes

Cooking Time: 10 minutes

Servings: 1

Ingredients:

1 lb. ground beef

6 slices cheddar cheese

6 dinner rolls

Salt and black pepper, to taste

Directions:

Preheat your air fryer to 390°F.

Form 6 beef patties, each about 2.5 oz., and season with salt and black pepper.

Add the burger patties to the cooking basket and cook them for 10 minutes.

Remove the burger patties from the air fryer, place the cheese on top of burgers, and return to the air fryer and cook for another minute.

Remove and put burgers on dinner rolls and serve warm.

Nutrition: Calories: 262, Total Fat: 9.4 g, Carbs: 8.2 g, Protein: 16.2 g

12. Avocado and Blueberry Muffins

Preparation Time: 10 minutes

Cooking Time: 15 minutes

Servings: 1

Ingredients:

2 eggs

1 cup blueberries

2 cups almond flour

1 tsp. baking soda

⅛ tsp. salt

2 ripe avocados, peeled, pitted, mashed

2 tbsp. liquid Stevia

1 cup plain Greek yogurt

1 tsp. vanilla extract

For the streusel topping:

2 tbsp. Truvia sweetener

4 tbsp. butter, softened

4 tbsp. almond flour

Directions:

Make the streusel topping by mixing Truvia, flour, and butter until you form a crumbly mixture. Place this mixture in the freezer for a while.

Meanwhile, make the muffins by sifting together flour, baking powder, baking soda, and salt, and set aside. Add avocados and liquid Stevia to a bowl and mix well. Adding in one egg at a time, continue to beat. Add the vanilla extract and yogurt and beat again.

Add in flour mixture a bit at a time and mix well. Add the blueberries into the mixture and gently fold them in. Pour the batter into greased muffin cups, then add the mixture until they are half-full.

Sprinkle the streusel topping mixture on top of the muffin mixture and place muffin cups in the air fryer basket.

Bake in the preheated air fryer at 355°F for 10 minutes. Remove the muffin cups from the air fryer and allow them to cool. Cool completely, then serve.

Nutrition: Calories: 202, Total Fat: 9.2 g, Carbs: 7.2 g, Protein: 6.3 g

13. Cheese Omelette

Preparation Time: 10 minutes

Cooking Time: 15 minutes

Servings: 1

Ingredients:

3 eggs

1 large yellow onion, diced

2 tbsp. cheddar cheese, shredded

½ tsp. soy sauce

Salt and pepper, to taste

Olive oil cooking spray

Directions:

In a container, whisk together eggs, soy sauce, pepper, and salt. Spray with olive oil cooking spray a small pan that will fit inside of your air fryer.

Transfer onions to the pan and spread them around. Air fry onions for 7 minutes.

Pour the beaten egg mixture over the cooked onions and sprinkle the top with shredded cheese.

Take back into the air fryer and cook for 6 minutes more.

Remove from the air fryer and serve Omelette with toasted multi-grain bread.

Nutrition: Calories: 232, Total Fat: 8.2 g, Carbs: 6.2 g, Protein: 12.3 g

14. Cauliflower Rice Bowls

Preparation time: 5 minutes

Cooking time: 15 minutes

Servings: 1

Ingredients:

12 ounces cauliflower rice

3 tablespoons stevia

2 tablespoons olive oil

2 tablespoons lime juice

1 pound fresh spinach, torn

1 red bell pepper, chopped

Directions:

In your air fryer, mix all the ingredients, toss, cook at 370 degrees F for 15 minutes, shaking halfway, divide between plates and serve for breakfast.

Nutrition: calories 219, fat 14, fiber 3, carbs 5, protein 7

15. Red Cabbage Bowls

Preparation time: 5 minutes

Cooking time: 15 minutes

Servings: 1

Ingredients:

2 cups red cabbage, shredded

A drizzle of olive oil

1 red bell pepper, sliced

1 small avocado, peeled, pitted and sliced

Salt and black pepper to the taste

Directions:

Grease your air fryer with the oil, add all the ingredients, toss, cover and cook at 400 degrees F for 15 minutes.

Divide into bowls and serve cold for breakfast.

Nutrition: calories 209, fat 8, fiber 2, carbs 4, protein 9

16.   Mixed Veggie Bake

Preparation time: 5 minutes

Cooking time: 20 minutes

Servings: 1

Ingredients:

2 garlic cloves, minced

1 teaspoon olive oil

2 celery stalks, chopped

½ cup white mushrooms, chopped

½ cup red bell pepper, chopped

Salt and black pepper to the taste

1 teaspoon oregano, dried

7 ounces mozzarella, shredded

1 tablespoon lemon juice

Directions:

Preheat the Air Fryer at 350 degrees F, add the oil and heat it up.

Add garlic, celery, mushrooms, bell pepper, salt, pepper, oregano, mozzarella and the lemon juice, toss and cook for 20 minutes.

Divide between plates and serve for breakfast.

Nutrition: calories 230, fat 11, fiber 2, carbs 4, protein 6

17.   Cinnamon Pudding

Preparation time: 4 minutes

Cooking time: 12 minutes

Servings: 1

Ingredients:

½ teaspoon cinnamon powder

¼ teaspoon allspice, ground

4 tablespoons erythritol

4 eggs, whisked

2 tablespoons heavy cream

Cooking spray

Directions:

In a bowl, mix all the ingredients except the cooking spray, whisk well and pour into a ramekin greased with cooking spray.

Add the basket to your Air Fryer, put the ramekin inside and cook at 400 degrees F for 12 minutes.

Divide into bowls and serve for breakfast.

Nutrition: calories 201, fat 11, fiber 2, carbs 4, protein 6

18. Paprika Broccoli and Eggs

Preparation time: 5 minutes

Cooking time: 20 minutes

Servings: 1

Ingredients:

1 broccoli head, florets separated and roughly chopped

Cooking spray

2 eggs, whisked

Salt and black pepper to the taste

1 tablespoon sweet paprika

4 ounces sour cream

Directions:

Grease a pan that fits your air fryer with the cooking spray and mix all the ingredients inside.

Put the pan in the Air Fryer and cook at 360 degrees F for 20 minutes.

Divide between plates and serve.

Nutrition: calories 220, fat 14, fiber 2, carbs 3, protein 2

19. Zucchini Fritters

Preparation time: 5 minutes

Cooking time: 8 minutes

Servings: 1

Ingredients:

8 ounces zucchinis, chopped

2 spring onions, chopped

2 eggs, whisked

Salt and black pepper to the taste

¼ teaspoon sweet paprika, chopped

Cooking spray

Directions:

In a bowl, mix all the ingredients except the cooking spray, stir well and shape medium fritters out of this mix.

Put the basket in the Air Fryer, add the fritters inside, grease them with cooking spray and cook at 400 degrees F for 8 minutes.

Divide the fritters between plates and serve for breakfast.

Nutrition: calories 202, fat 10, fiber 2, carbs 4, protein 5

20. Broccoli Cheese Quiche

Preparation Time: 10 minutes

Cooking Time: 40 minutes

Servings: 1

Ingredients:

1 large broccoli, chopped into florets

3 large carrots, peeled and diced

1 cup cheddar cheese, grated

¼ cup feta cheese

2 large eggs

1 teaspoon dried rosemary

1 teaspoon dried thyme

Salt and black pepper, to taste

Directions:

Preheat the Air fryer to 360 o F and grease a quiche dish.

Place broccoli and carrots into a food steamer and cook for about 20 minutes until soft.

Whisk together eggs with milk, dried herbs, salt and black pepper in a bowl.

Place steamed vegetables at the bottom of the quiche pan and top with tomatoes and cheese.

Drizzle with the egg mixture and transfer the quiche dish in the Air fryer.

Cook for about 20 minutes and dish out to serve warm.

Nutrition: Calories: 412, Fat: 28, Carbohydrates: 16.3g, Sugar: 7.5g, Protein: 25.3g, Sodium: 720mg

21.   Bacon and Egg Bite Cups

Preparation Time: 15 minutes

Cooking Time: 15 minutes

Servings: 1

Ingredients:

6 large eggs

½ cup red peppers, chopped

¼ cup fresh spinach, chopped

¾ cup mozzarella cheese, shredded

3 slices bacon, cooked and crumbled

2 tablespoons heavy whipping cream

Salt and black pepper, to taste

Directions:

Preheat the Air fryer to 300 o F and grease 4 silicone molds.

Whisk together eggs with cream, salt and black pepper in a large bowl until combined.

Stir in rest of the ingredients and transfer the mixture into silicone molds.

Place in the Air fryer and cook for about 15 minutes.

Dish out and serve warm.

Nutrition: Calories: 233, Fats: 17.2g, Carbohydrates: 2.9g, Sugar: 1.6g, Proteins: 16.8g, Sodium: 472mg

22.   Air Fryer Sausage

Preparation Time: 5 minutes

Cooking Time: 20 minutes

Servings: 1

Ingredients:

5 raw and uncooked sausage links

1 tablespoon olive oil

Directions:

Preheat the Air fryer to 360 o F and grease an Air fryer basket with olive oil.

Cook for about 15 minutes and flip the sausages.

Cook for 5 more minutes and serve warm.

Nutrition: Calories: 131, Fat: 11.8g, Carbohydrates: 0g, Sugar: 0g, Protein: 6g, Sodium: 160mg

23.   Bacon Grilled Cheese

Preparation Time: 5 minutes

Cooking Time: 7 minutes

Servings: 1

Ingredients:

4 slices of bread

1 tablespoon butter, softened

2 slices mild cheddar cheese

6 slices bacon, cooked

2 slices mozzarella cheese

1 tablespoon olive oil

Directions:

Preheat the Air fryer to 370 o F and grease an Air fryer basket with olive oil.

Spread butter onto one side of each bread slice and place in the Air Fryer basket.

Layer with cheddar cheese slice, followed by bacon, mozzarella cheese and close with the other bread slice.

Place in the Air fryer and cook for about 4 minutes.

Flip the sandwich and cook for 3 more minutes.

Remove from the Air fryer and serve.

Nutrition: Calories: 518, Fat: 34.9g, Carbohydrates: 20g, Sugar: 0.6g, Protein: 29.9g, Sodium: 1475mg

CHAPTER 2: LUNCH RECIPES

24. Crusted Chicken Drumsticks

Preparation Time: 10 minutes

Cooking Time: 10 minutes

Servings: 1

Ingredients:

1 lb. chicken drumsticks

1/2 cup buttermilk

1/2 cup panko breadcrumbs

1/2 cup flour

1/4 tsp. baking powder

Spice Mixture:

1/2 tsp. salt

1/2 tsp. celery salt

1/4 tsp. oregano

1/4 tsp. cayenne

1 tsp. paprika

1/4 tsp. garlic powder

1/4 tsp. dried thyme

1/2 tsp. ground ginger

1/2 tsp. white pepper

1/2 tsp. black pepper

3 tbsp. butter melted

Directions:

1. Soak chicken in the buttermilk and cover to marinate overnight in the refrigerator — mix spices with flour, breadcrumbs, and baking powder in a shallow tray.

2. Remove the chicken from the milk and coat them well with the flour spice mixture.

3. Place the chicken drumsticks in the Air fryer basket of the Ninja Oven.

4. Pour the melted butter over the drumsticks.

5. Turn the dial to select the "Air fry" mode. Hit the Time button and again use the dial to set the cooking time to 10 minutes.

6. Now push the Temp button and rotate the dial to set the temperature at 425 degrees F.

7. Once preheated, place the baking tray inside the oven.

8. Flip the drumsticks and resume cooking for another 10 minutes.

9. Serve warm.

Nutrition:

Calories: 331 kcal

Fat: 2.5g

Carbs: 69g

Protein: 28.7g

25. Lemony Salmon

Preparation Time: 5 minutes

Cooking Time: 10 minutes

Servings: 1

Ingredients:

1 tbsp. of fresh lemon juice

½ tbsp. olive oil

Salt and ground black pepper, as required

1 garlic clove, minced

½ tsp. fresh thyme leaves, chopped

2 (7-oz) salmon fillets

Directions:

1. In a container, add all ingredients except the salmon and mix well. Add the salmon fillets and coat with the mixture generously.

2. Arrange the salmon fillets onto a lightly greased cooking rack, skin-side down. Arrange the drip pan in the bottom of the Instant Vortex Air Fryer Oven cooking chamber. Select "Air Fry" and then adjust the temperature to 400 °F. Set the time for 10 minutes and press "Start."

3. When the display shows "Add Food," insert the cooking rack in the bottom position, the display shows "Turn Food" turn the fillets.

4. When the cooking time is complete, remove the tray from the Vortex Oven. Serve hot.

Nutrition:

Calories: 297 kcal

Carbs: 0.8g

Fat: 15.8g

Protein: 38.7g

26.   BBQ Turkey Meatballs with Cranberry Sauce

Preparation Time: 5 minutes

Cooking Time: 20 minutes

Servings: 1

Ingredients:

1 ½ tbsp. water

2 tsp. cider vinegar

1 tsp. salt and more to taste

1-pound ground turkey

1 1/2 tbsp. barbecue sauce

1/3 cup cranberry sauce

1/4-pound ground bacon

Directions:

1. In a container, mix with hands the turkey, ground bacon, and a tsp. of salt. Evenly form into 16 equal-sized balls.

2. In a small saucepan, boil cranberry sauce, barbecue sauce, water, cider vinegar, and a dash or two of salt. Mix well and simmer for 3 minutes.

3. Thread meatballs in skewers and baste with cranberry sauce. Place on skewer rack in the air fryer.

4. For 15 minutes, cook it on 360oF. Every after 5 minutes of cooking time, turnover skewers and baste with sauce. If needed, cook in batches.

5. Serve and enjoy.

Nutrition:

Calories: 217 kcal

Carbs: 11.5g

Protein: 28.0g

Fat: 10.9g

27. Beef & veggie Spring Rolls

Preparation Time: 5 minutes

Cooking Time: 12 minutes

Servings: 1

Ingredients:

2-ounce Asian rice noodles

1 tbsp. sesame oil

7-ounce ground beef

1 small onion, chopped

3 garlic cloves, crushed

1 cup fresh mixed vegetables

1 tsp. soy sauce

1 packet spring roll skins

2 tbsp. water

Olive oil, as required

Directions:

1. Soak the noodles in warm water till soft.

2. Dry out and cut into small lengths. In a pan, heat the oil and add the onion and garlic and sauté for about 4-5 minutes.

3. Add beef and cook for about 4-5 minutes.

4. Add vegetables and cook for about 5-7 minutes or until cooked.

5. Stir in soy sauce and remove from the heat.

6. Immediately stir in the noodles and keep aside till all the juices have been absorbed.

7. Preheat the Air Fryer Oven to 350 degrees F.

8. Place the spring rolls skin onto a smooth surface.

9. Add a line of the filling diagonally across.

10. Fold the top point over the filling and then fold in both sides.

11. On the final point, brush it with water before rolling to seal.

12. Brush the spring rolls with oil.

13. Arrange the rolls in batches in the air fryer and cook for about 8 minutes

14. Repeat with remaining rolls. Now, place spring rolls onto a baking sheet.

15. Bake it for about 6 minutes per side.

Nutrition:

Calories: 364 kcal

Fat: 9g

Carbs: 39g

Protein: 32g

28. Lemon Garlic Shrimp

Preparation Time: 5 minutes

Cooking Time: 5 minutes

Servings: 1

Ingredients:

1-pound small shrimp, peeled with tails removed

1 tbsp. olive oil

4 garlic cloves, minced

1 lemon, zested and juiced

1 pinch crushed red pepper flakes (optional)

1/4 cup parsley, chopped

1/4 tsp. sea salt

Directions:

1. Preheat vortex air fryer to 400 ° F.

2. In a container, mix the shrimp, olive oil, garlic, salt, lemon zest, and pepper flakes (whether used). Mix to cover.

3. Put the shrimp in the basket of your air fryer oven. Cook for 6-7 minutes, until the shrimps are done, pour the shrimps into a container and mix them with lemon juice and parsley. Season with additional salt.

Nutrition:

Calories: 130 kcal

Fat: 4.6g

Carbs: 4.7g

Protein: 20.3g

29. Parsley Catfish

Preparation Time: 10 minutes

Cooking Time: 25 minutes

Servings: 1

Ingredients:

4 catfish fillets

1/4 cup Louisiana Fish fry

1 tbsp. olive oil

1 tbsp. chopped parsley optional

1 lemon, sliced

Fresh herbs to garnish

Directions:

1. First, Preheat the air fryer to 400 degrees F.

2. Rinse the fish fillets and pat them try.

3. Rub the fillets with the seasoning and coat well.

4. Spray oil on top of each fillet.

5. Place the fillets in the air fryer basket.

6. Cover the lid and cook for 10 minutes.

7. Flip the fillets and cook more for another 10 minutes.

8. Flip the fish and cook for 3 minutes until crispy.

9. Garnish with parsley, fresh herbs, and lemon. Serve warm.

Nutrition:

Calories: 248 kcal

Fat: 15.7g

Carbs: 0.4g

Protein: 24.9g

30. Easy Italian Meatballs

Preparation Time: 10 minutes

Cooking Time: 13 minutes

Servings: 1

Ingredients:

2-lb. lean ground turkey

¼ cup onion, minced

2 cloves garlic, minced

2 tbsp. parsley, chopped

2 eggs

1½ cup parmesan cheese, grated

½ tsp. red pepper flakes

½ tsp. Italian seasoning

Salt and black pepper to taste

Directions:

1. Toss all the meatball ingredients in a bowl and mix well. Make small meatballs out of this mixture and place them in the air fryer basket.

2. Press the "Power Button" of the Air Fry Oven and turn the dial to select the "Air Fry" mode. Press the Time button and again turn the dial to set the cooking time to 13 minutes. Now push the Temp button and rotate the dial to set the temperature at 350 degrees F.

3. Once preheated, place the air fryer basket inside and close its lid.

4. Flip the meatballs when cooked halfway through.

5. Serve warm.

Nutrition:

Calories: 472 kcal

Fat: 25.8g

Carbs: 1.7g

Protein: 59.6g

31. Crispy Haddock

Preparation Time: 5 minutes

Cooking Time: 10 minutes

Servings: 1

Ingredients:

½ cup flour

½ tsp. paprika

1 egg, beaten

¼ cup mayonnaise

4 oz salt and vinegar potato chips, crushed finely

1 lb. haddock fillet cut into 6 pieces

Direction:

1. In a shallow container, mix together the flour and paprika. In a second shallow dish, add the egg and mayonnaise and beat well. In a third shallow dish, place the crushed potato chips.

2. Coat the fish pieces with flour mixture, then dip into the egg mixture, and finally coat with the potato chips. Arrange the fish pieces onto 2 cooking trays.

3. Arrange the drip pan in the bottom of the Instant Vortex Air Fryer Oven cooking chamber. Select "Air Fry" and then adjust the temperature to 370 °F. Set the time for 10 minutes and press "Start."

4. When the display shows "Add Food," insert 1 cooking tray in the top position and another in the bottom part.

5. When the display shows "Turn Food," do not turn the food but switch the position of cooking trays. When cooking time is complete, remove the trays from the Vortex Oven. Serve hot.

Nutrition:

Calories: 456 kcal

Carbs: 40.9g

Fat: 22.7g

Protein: 43.5g

32. Fennel and Tomato Stew

Preparation Time: 25 minutes

Cooking Time: 25 minutes

Servings: 1

Ingredients:

2 fennel bulbs; shredded

½ cup chicken stock

1 red bell pepper; chopped.

2 garlic cloves; minced

2 cups tomatoes; cubed

2 tbsp. tomato puree

1 tsp. rosemary; dried

1 tsp. sweet paprika

Salt and black pepper to taste.

Directions:

In a pan that fits your air fryer, mix all the ingredients, toss, introduce in the fryer and cook at 380°F for 15 minutes

Divide the stew into bowls.

Nutrition: Calories: 184; Fat: 7g; Fiber: 2g; Carbs: 3g; Protein: 8g

33. Spinach and Olives

Preparation Time: 25 minutes

Cooking Time: 20 minutes

Servings: 1

Ingredients:

½ cup tomato puree

4 cups spinach; torn

2 cups black olives, pitted and halved

3 celery stalks; chopped.

1 red bell pepper; chopped.

2 tomatoes; chopped.

Salt and black pepper to taste.

Directions:

In a pan that fits your air fryer, mix all the ingredients except the spinach, toss, introduce the pan in the air fryer and cook at 370°F for 15 minutes

Add the spinach, toss, cook for 5 - 6 minutes more, divide into bowls and serve.

Nutrition: Calories: 193; Fat: 6g; Fiber: 2g; Carbs: 4g; Protein: 6g

34. Turkey and Broccoli Stew

Preparation Time: 30 minutes

Cooking Time: 15 minutes

Servings: 1

Ingredients:

1 broccoli head, florets separated

1 turkey breast, skinless; boneless and cubed

1 cup tomato sauce

1 tbsp. parsley; chopped.

1 tbsp. olive oil

Salt and black pepper to taste.

Directions:

In a baking dish that fits your air fryer, mix the turkey with the rest of the ingredients except the parsley, toss, introduce the dish in the fryer, bake at 380°F for 25 minutes

Divide into bowls, sprinkle the parsley on top and serve.

Nutrition: Calories: 250; Fat: 11g; Fiber: 2g; Carbs: 6g; Protein: 12g

35. Zucchini Stew

Preparation Time: 17 minutes

Cooking Time: 25 minutes

Servings: 1

Ingredients:

8 zucchinis, roughly cubed

¼ cup tomato sauce

1 tbsp. olive oil

½ tsp. basil; chopped.

¼ tsp. rosemary; dried

Salt and black pepper to taste.

Directions:

Grease a pan that fits your air fryer with the oil, add all the ingredients, toss, introduce the pan in the fryer and cook at 350°F for 12 minutes

Divide into bowls and serve.

Nutrition: Calories: 200; Fat: 6g; Fiber: 2g; Carbs: 4g; Protein: 6g

36.   Pork Stew

Preparation Time: 35 minutes

Cooking Time: 26 minutes

Servings: 1

Ingredients:

2 lb. pork stew meat; cubed

1 eggplant; cubed

½ cup beef stock

2 zucchinis; cubed

½ tsp. smoked paprika

Salt and black pepper to taste.

A handful cilantro; chopped.

Directions:

In a pan that fits your air fryer, mix all the ingredients, toss, introduce in your air fryer and cook at 370°F for 30 minutes

Divide into bowls and serve right away.

Nutrition: Calories: 245; Fat: 12g; Fiber: 2g; Carbs: 5g; Protein: 14g

37. Chicken and Celery Stew

Preparation Time: 35 minutes

Cooking Time: 30 minutes

Servings: 1

Ingredients:

1 lb. chicken breasts, skinless; boneless and cubed

4 celery stalks; chopped.

½ cup coconut cream

2 red bell peppers; chopped.

2 tsp. garlic; minced

1 tbsp. butter, soft

Salt and black pepper to taste.

Directions:

Grease a baking dish that fits your air fryer with the butter, add all the ingredients in the pan and toss them.

Introduce the dish in the fryer, cook at 360°F for 30 minutes, divide into bowls and serve

Nutrition: Calories: 246; Fat: 12g; Fiber: 2g; Carbs: 6g; Protein: 12g

38. Okra and Green Beans Stew

Preparation Time: 20 minutes

Cooking Time: 15 minutes

Servings: 1

Ingredients:

1 lb. green beans; halved

4 garlic cloves; minced

1 cup okra

3 tbsp. tomato sauce

1 tbsp. thyme; chopped.

Salt and black pepper to taste.

Directions:

In a pan that fits your air fryer, mix all the ingredients, toss, introduce the pan in the air fryer and cook at 370°F for 15 minutes

Divide the stew into bowls and serve.

Nutrition: Calories: 183; Fat: 5g; Fiber: 2g; Carbs: 4g; Protein: 8g

39. Chimichurri Skirt Steak

Preparation Time: 10 minutes

Cooking Time: 8 minutes

Servings: 1

Ingredients:

2 x 8 oz. skirt steak

1 cup finely chopped parsley

¼ cup finely chopped mint

2 tbsp. fresh oregano (washed & finely chopped)

3 finely chopped cloves of garlic

1 tsp. red pepper flakes (crushed)

1 tbsp. ground cumin

1 tsp. cayenne pepper

2 tsp. smoked paprika

1 tsp. salt

¼ tsp. pepper

¾ cup oil

3 tbsp. red wine vinegar

Directions:

1. Toss all the ingredients in a container (besides the steak) and mix well.

2. Put ¼ cup of the mixture in a plastic baggie with the steak and leave it in the fridge overnight (2-24hrs).

3. Leave the bag out at room temperature for at least 30 min before popping it into the air fryer. Preheat for a minute or two to 390° F before cooking until med–rare (8–10 min). Pour into the Oven rack/basket. Place the Rack on the middle-shelf of the Air Fryer Oven. Set temperature to 390°F, and set time to 10 minutes

4. Put 2 tbsp. ff the chimichurri mix on top of each steak before serving.

Nutrition:

Calories: 308.6 kcal

Fat: 22.6g

Carbs: 3g

Protein: 23.7g

40.   Air Fryer Buffalo Mushroom Poppers

Preparation Time: 30 minutes

Cooking Time: 50 minutes

Servings: 1

Ingredients:

1-pound fresh whole button mushrooms

1/2 tsp. kosher salt

3 tbsp. 1/3-less-fat cream cheese,

1/4 cup all-purpose flour

Softened 1 jalapeño chili, seeded and minced

Cooking spray

1/2 cup crumbled blue cheese

1 cup panko breadcrumbs

2 large eggs, lightly beaten

1/4 cup buffalo-style hot sauce

2 tbsp. chopped fresh chives

1/4 tsp. black pepper

1/2 cup plain fat-free yogurt

1/2 cup low-fat buttermilk

3 tbsp. apple cider vinegar

Directions:

1. Chop the stems Removed from the mushroom caps and set them aside. Stir the mushroom stems, cream cheese, jalapeño, salt, and pepper together. Stuff about 1 tsp of the mixture into each mushroom cap, rounding the filling to form a smooth ball.

2. Place panko in a bowl and the flour in a second bowl, and eggs in third Coat mushrooms in the flour, dip in egg mixture, and dredge in panko, pressing to adhere. Spray mushrooms well with cooking spray.

3. Put half of the sprayed mushrooms in an air fryer basket, and cook for 20 minutes at 350°F. Transfer cooked mushrooms to a large bowl. Drizzle with buffalo sauce over mushrooms; toss to coat, then sprinkle with chives.

4. Stir buttermilk, yogurt, blue cheese, and cider vinegar in a small bowl. Serve mushroom poppers with blue cheese sauce.

Nutrition:

Calories: 133 kcal

Fat: 4g

Protein: 7g

Carbs: 16g

41.   Cabbage and Radishes Mix

Preparation Time: 20 minutes

Cooking Time: 8 minutes

Servings: 1

Ingredients:

6 cups green cabbage; shredded

½ cup celery leaves; chopped.

¼ cup green onions; chopped.

6 radishes; sliced

3 tbsp. olive oil

2 tbsp. balsamic vinegar

½ tsp. hot paprika

1 tsp. lemon juice

Directions:

In your air fryer's pan, combine all the ingredients and toss well.

Introduce the pan in the fryer and cook at 380°F for 15 minutes. Divide between plates and serve as a side dish

Nutrition: Calories: 130; Fat: 4g; Fiber: 3g; Carbs: 4g; Protein: 7g

42. Charred Bell Peppers

Preparation Time: 6 minutes

Cooking Time: 4 minutes

Servings: 1

Ingredients:

1 lemon

1 pinch sea salt

1 teaspoon olive oil

20 bell peppers, sliced and seeded

Directions:

Heat the air fryer to 390°F.

Season the peppers with oil and salt.

Place peppers in the air fryer and cook for 4 minutes.

Place peppers on a plate and season with salt, pepper, and lemon juice.

Nutrition:

Calories: 30

Fat: 0.25 g

Carbohydrates: 6.91 g

Protein: 1.28 g

43. Garlic Tomatoes

Preparation Time: 7 minutes

Cooking Time: 15 minutes

Servings: 1

Ingredients:

3 tbsp vinegar

4 tomatoes

1 tbsp olive oil

Salt and black pepper to season

1 garlic clove, minced

1/2 tsp thyme, dried

Directions:

Heat the air fryer to 390°F.

Cut the tomatoes in half and carefully remove the seeds. Season them in a large bowl with oil, pepper, garlic, salt, and thyme.

Cook them in the air fryer for 15 minutes.

Serve them by adding vinegar.

Nutrition:

Calories: 28.9

Fat: 2.4 g

Carbohydrates: 2.0 g

Protein: 0.4 g

44. Cauliflower Fritters

Preparation Time: 10 minutes

Cooking Time: 15 minutes

Servings: 1

Ingredients:

5 cups chopped cauliflower florets

1/2 tsp ground black pepper

1/2 tsp salt

2 eggs

1/2 cup almond flour

1/2 tsp baking powder

Directions:

Cut the cauliflower into small pieces and blend it into a food processor. Pour the mixture into a bowl.

Add the remaining ingredients and mix well. Form into patties.

Preheat the air fryer to 390 degrees for 5 minutes.

Add cauliflower patties and spray with oil. Cook for 15 minutes until golden brown, turning patties halfway through cooking.

Serve.

Nutrition:

Calories: 272 Cal

Carbs: 57 g

Fat: 0.3 g

Protein: 11 g

Fiber: 8 g

45. Spiced Nuts

Preparation Time: 3 minutes

Cooking Time: 20 minutes

Servings: 1

Ingredients:

1 cup almonds

1 cup cashews

1 cup pecan halves

1 egg white, beaten

1/2 tsp cinnamon, ground

1/4 tsp cloves, ground

Dash salt

Pinch cayenne pepper

Directions:

In a bowl, combine the egg white with the spices.

Heat the air fryer to 300°F.

Toss the nuts in the spice mixture and cook them for about 20 minutes.

Stir several times during cooking.

Nutrition:

Calories: 88

Fat: 7 g

Carbohydrates: 3.1 g

Protein: 3.5 g

46. Garlic Cauliflower Tots

Preparation Time: 5 minutes

Cooking Time: 20 minutes

Servings: 6

Ingredients:

1 crown cauliflower, chopped in a food processor

1/2 cup parmesan cheese, grated

Salt and pepper to season

1/4 cup almond flour

2 eggs

1 teaspoon garlic, minced

Directions:

Preheat the air fryer to 400°F.

Mix all ingredients in a bowl and form small croquettes.

Place the balls in the fryer and drizzle with olive oil.

Cook for 20 and turn them over halfway through cooking.

Nutrition:

Calories: 17

Fat: 0.5 g

Carbohydrates: 1.1 g

Protein: 1.8 g

47. Coriander Artichokes

Preparation Time: 20 minutes

Cooking Time: 15 minutes

Servings: 1

Ingredients:

12 oz. artichoke hearts

1 tbsp. lemon juice

1 tsp. coriander, ground

½ tsp. cumin seeds

½ tsp. olive oil

Salt and black pepper to taste.

Directions:

In a pan that fits your air fryer, mix all the ingredients, toss, introduce the pan in the fryer and cook at 370°F for 15 minutes

Divide the mix between plates and serve as a side dish.

Nutrition: Calories: 200; Fat: 7g; Fiber: 2g; Carbs: 5g; Protein: 8g

48. Spinach and Artichokes Sauté

Preparation Time: 20 minutes

Cooking Time: 25 minutes

Servings: 1

Ingredients:

10 oz. artichoke hearts; halved

2 cups baby spinach

3 garlic cloves

¼ cup veggie stock

2 tsp. lime juice

Salt and black pepper to taste.

Directions:

In a pan that fits your air fryer, mix all the ingredients, toss, introduce in the fryer and cook at 370°F for 15 minutes

Divide between plates and serve as a side dish.

Nutrition: Calories: 209; Fat: 6g; Fiber: 2g; Carbs: 4g; Protein: 8g

CHAPTER 3: DINNER RECIPES

49. Parmesan Shrimp

Preparation Time: 10 minutes

Cooking Time: 10 minutes

Servings: 1

Ingredients:

2 pounds jumbo shrimp, wild-caught, peeled, deveined

2 tbsp. minced garlic

1 tsp. onion powder

1 tsp. basil

1 tsp. ground black pepper

1/2 tsp. dried oregano

2 tbsp. olive oil

2/3 cup grated parmesan cheese

2 tbsp. lemon juice

Directions:

1. Switch on the air fryer, insert fryer basket, grease it with olive oil, then shut with its lid, set the fryer at 350 degrees F, and preheat for 5 minutes.

2. Meanwhile, place cheese in a bowl, add remaining ingredients except for shrimps and lemon juice and stir until combined.

3. Add shrimps and then toss until well coated.

4. Open the fryer, add shrimps in it, spray oil over them, close with its lid and cook for 10 minutes until nicely golden and crispy, shaking halfway through the frying. When the air fryer beeps, open its lid, transfer chicken onto a serving plate, Drizzle with lemon juice and serve.

Nutrition:

Calories: 307 kcal

Carbs: 12g

Fat: 16.4g

Protein: 27.6g

50. Tuna Chipotle

Preparation Time: 5 minutes

Cooking Time: 8 minutes

Servings: 1

Ingredients:

142g tuna

45g chipotle sauce

4 slices white bread

2 slices pepper jack cheese

Directions:

1. Preheat the air fryer set the temperature to 160°C. Mix the tuna and chipotle until combined.

2. Spread half of the chipotle tuna mixture on each of the 2 slices of bread.

3. Add a piece of pepper jack cheese on each and close with the remaining 2 slices of bread, making 2 sandwiches.

4. Place the sandwiches in the preheated air fryer. Set the timer to 8 minutes.

5. Cut diagonally and serve.

Nutrition:

Calories: 121 kcal

Fat: 4g

Carbs: 2g

Protein: 16g

51. Spicy Duck Legs

Preparation Time: 5 minutes

Cooking Time: 30 minutes

Servings: 1

Ingredients:

2 duck legs, bone-in, and skin on

Salt and pepper

1 tsp. five-spice powder

1 tbsp. herbs that you like such as thyme, parsley, etc., chopped

Directions:

1. Rub the spices over duck legs.

2. Place duck legs in the air fryer and cook for 25-minutes at 325°Fahrenheit.

3. Then air fry them at 400°Fahrenheit for 5-minutes

Nutrition:

Calories: 207 kcal

Fat: 10.6g

Carbs: 1.9g

Protein: 25g

52.   Thai Sweet Chili Garlic Shrimp

Preparation Time: 10 minutes

Cooking Time: 10 minutes

Servings: 1

Ingredients:

For shrimp:

1 egg

12-15 medium shrimps (with shells)

30g tapioca flour

For sauce:

1 tbsp. olive oil

1 tbsp. garlic

3 tbsp. Thai sweet chili sauce

2 tbsp. lime juice

2 tsp. brown sugar

1 tsp. chili pepper

2 tsp. cilantro

Directions:

1. First, you should line your air fryer basket with a sheet of lightly greased aluminum foil.

2. Beat the egg until thoroughly mixed, dip the shrimps into the egg, then dip them into the tapioca flour, ensuring that they are evenly covered. Place into the air fryer basket. Spray with cooking oil and cook at 380 degrees Fahrenheit for 6 to 7 minutes, flipping once in the middle. Remove once fully cooked through.

3. While the shrimps cook, mince the garlic and add to a wok with olive oil for about one minute until softened. Add the Thai sweet chili sauce, lime juice, brown sugar, and chili pepper, and stir until the sauce has thickened. Once the shrimps are cooked, add to the sauce and coat.

4. Garnish the shrimps with cilantro to serve.

Nutrition:

Calories: 129 kcal

Fat: 5g

Carbs: 16g

Protein: 5g

53. Lemon Chili Prawns

Preparation Time: 8 minutes

Cooking Time: 15 minutes

Servings: 1

Ingredients:

250g prawns

Pinch salt

½ tbsp. ginger garlic paste

5ml lemon juice

5g chili garlic paste

50g hung curd

A dash soya sauce

10ml cooking oil

Directions:

1. Remove the veins from the prawns and wash them.

2. In a bowl, mix together the salt, ginger garlic paste, lemon juice, chili garlic paste, hung curd, and the soya sauce. Marinate the prawns in the sauce. Leave for one hour.

3. Preheat the air fryer to 400 degrees Fahrenheit. Using the cooking oil coat the base of the air fryer.

4. Put the prawns into the basket and coat lightly with the oil. Cook the prawns for 6 minutes. Turnover and cook for another 6 minutes.

Nutrition:

Calories: 148 kcal

Fat: 4.7g

Carbs: 2.4g

Protein: 22.7g

54. Lemony and Spicy Coconut Crusted Salmon

Preparation Time: 10 minutes

Cooking Time: 6 minutes

Servings: 1

Ingredients:

1 pound salmon

½ cup flour

2 egg whites

½ cup breadcrumbs

½ cup unsweetened coconut, shredded

¼ teaspoon lemon zest

Salt and freshly ground black pepper, to taste

¼ teaspoon cayenne pepper

¼ teaspoon red pepper flakes, crushed

Vegetable oil, as required

Directions:

Preheat the Air fryer to 400 o F and grease an Air fryer basket.

Mix the flour, salt and black pepper in a shallow dish.

Whisk the egg whites in a second shallow dish.

Mix the breadcrumbs, coconut, lime zest, salt and cayenne pepper in a third shallow dish.

Coat salmon in the flour, then dip in the egg whites and then into the breadcrumb mixture evenly.

Place the salmon in the Air fryer basket and drizzle with vegetable oil.

Cook for about 6 minutes and dish out to serve warm.

Nutrition: Calories: 558, Fat: 22.2g, Carbohydrates: 18.6g, Sugar: 8.7g, Protein: 43g, Sodium: 3456mg

55. Green Onions & Parmesan Tomatoes

Preparation Time: 5 minutes

Cooking Time: 15 minutes

Servings: 1

Ingredients:

1 tbsp olive oil

1/2 cup parmesan, grated

1/2 tsp thyme, dried

2 garlic cloves, minced

2 green onions, chopped

4 large tomatoes, cut into slices

Salt and pepper to season

Directions:

Heat the air fryer to 390°F.

Season tomato slices with garlic, olive oil, thyme, salt, and pepper. Top with chopped green onions and Parmesan cheese.

Place tomatoes in the air fryer basket and cook for about 15 minutes.

Serve.

Nutrition:

Calories: 68

Fat: 3.8 g

Carbohydrates: 68 g

Protein: 1.9 g

56. Green Bell Peppers with Cauliflower Stuffing

Preparation Time: 10 minutes

Cooking Time: 20 minutes

Servings: 1

Ingredients:

1 tsp cumin seeds

1 tsp lemon juice

1/4 tsp chili powder

1/4 tsp garam masala

1/4 tsp turmeric powder

2 cups cauliflower, cooked and mashed

2 green chilies, chopped

2 onions, chopped

2 tablespoons coriander leaves, chopped

4 green bell peppers, deseeded

Olive oil as needed

Salt to season

Directions:

Sauté the chilies, onion, and cumin seeds in a pot with oil.

Add the rest of the ingredients, except the peppers, and mix well.

Heat the air fryer to 390°F.

Brush the green peppers with olive oil and stuff them with the cauliflower mixture.

Place them in the air fryer basket and grill for 10 minutes.

Nutrition:

Calories: 256

Fat: 4.0 g

Carbohydrates: 41.8 g

Protein: 12.3 g

57. Cheesy Chickpea & Courgetti Burgers

Preparation Time: 7 minutes

Cooking Time: 15 minutes

Servings: 1

Ingredients:

1 can chickpeas, drained

1 red onion, diced

1 tsp chili powder

1 tsp cumin

1 tsp garlic puree

1 tsp spice, mixed

1 zucchini, spiralizer

1-ounce cheddar cheese, shredded

2 eggs, beaten

3 tbsp coriander

Salt and pepper to season

Directions:

Mix ingredients in a bowl and form small burgers.

Place in the air fryer at 300°F for 15 minutes.

Nutrition:

Calories: 171

Fat: 10.1 g

Carbohydrates: 18.4 g

Protein: 13.2 g

58. Spicy Sweet Potatoes

Preparation Time: 5 minutes

Cooking Time: 23 minutes

Servings: 1

Ingredients:

1 onion, peeled and diced

1 tbsp red wine vinegar

1 tomato, thinly sliced

1 tsp chili powder

1 tsp oregano

1 tsp paprika

1 tsp rosemary

1 tsp spice, mixed

1/2 cup tomato sauce

2 tbsp olive oil

2 tsp coriander

2 tsp thyme

3 sweet potatoes, peeled and chopped into chips

Salt and pepper to season

Directions:

In a bowl, grease the chips with olive oil and cook them in the air fryer for about 15 minutes at 360°F.

Carefully mix the remaining ingredients in a second bowl.

Pour the sauce into the air fryer for about 8 minutes as well.

Serve the potatoes with the sauce.

Nutrition:

Calories: 293

Fat: 5 g

Carbohydrates: 51 g

Protein: 8 g

59.   Rice in Crab Shell

Preparation Time: 20 minutes

Cooking Time: 8 minutes

Servings: 1

Ingredients:

1 bowl cooked rice

4 tablespoons crab meat

2 tablespoons butter

2 tablespoons Parmesan cheese, shredded

2 crab shells

Paprika, to taste

Directions:

Preheat the Air fryer to 390 o F and grease an Air fryer basket.

Mix rice, crab meat, butter and paprika in a bowl.

Fill crab shell with rice mixture and top with Parmesan cheese.

Arrange the crab shell in the Air fryer basket and cook for about 8 minutes.

Sprinkle with more paprika and serve hot.

Nutrition: Calories: 285, Fat: 33g, Carbohydrates: 0g, Sugar: 0g, Protein: 33g, Sodium: 153mg

60. Crab Fingers

Preparation time: 15 minutes

Cooking time: 10 minutes

Servings: 1

Ingredients:

8 oz crab meat

2 tablespoons almond flour

1 egg, beaten

1 teaspoon chili pepper

½ teaspoon chili powder

1 teaspoon dried oregano

1 teaspoon ground coriander

½ teaspoon paprika

2 tablespoons lime juice

1 teaspoon olive oil

Directions:

Place the crab meat in the big bowl and churn it with the help of the fork.

After this, add almond flour, chili pepper, chili powder, dried oregano, ground coriander, and paprika.

Make the medium "fingers" from the crab mixture and sprinkle every with bread crumbs.

Transfer the fingers in the air fryer and sprinkle with olive oil.

Close the lid.

Cook the crab fingers for 5 minutes from each side at 380F or until golden brown.

Nutrition: calories 190, fat 7.2, fiber 1.2, carbs 9.5, protein 18.2

61. Saba Fish

Preparation time: 15 minutes

Cooking time: 9 minutes

Servings: 1

Ingredients:

14 oz mackerel, fillet

1 teaspoon chili flakes

2 tablespoons coconut ream

1 teaspoon ground paprika

1 tablespoon almond flour

1 teaspoon tomato paste

1 teaspoon avocado oil

½ teaspoon salt

Directions:

In the mixing bowl combine together chili flakes, ground paprika, and salt.

Then rub the fillet with spice mixture well.

After this, rub the mackerel with tomato paste and coconut cream and coat in the corn flour.

Sprinkle the fish with avocado oil and arrange in the air fryer.

Close the lid and cook fish fillet for 5 minutes at 385F.

After this, flip the fish on another side.

Close the lid and cook it for 4 minutes more.

Nutrition: calories 303, fat 20.6, fiber 0.4, carbs 2.3, protein 25.8

62. African Tilapia

Preparation time: 25 minutes

Cooking time: 10 minutes

Servings: 1

Ingredients:

12 oz tilapia, trimmed

1 lemon

1 teaspoon ground black pepper

½ teaspoon ground nutmeg

½ teaspoon white pepper

2 garlic cloves, peeled, diced

1 teaspoon ground paprika

½ teaspoon minced ginger

¼ cup fresh parsley, chopped

¼ white onion, peeled, chopped

½ teaspoon anise seeds

1 tablespoon olive oil

4 tablespoons water

Directions:

Make the diagonal cuts in the tilapia.

Then rub the fish with ground black pepper, nutmeg, and white pepper.

After this, in the mixing bowl combine together garlic cloves, ground paprika, minced ginger, parsley, onion, and anise seeds. Add olive oil and water and stir until homogenous.

Grind the mixture until smooth.

Then squeeze the juice over the tilapia and massage it with the help of the fingertips.

After this, rub the fish generously with the grinded mixture and transfer in the air fryer. Leave it for 10-15 minutes to marinate.

Close the lid and cook the tilapia for 5 minutes from each side at 395F.

Nutrition: calories 117, fat 4.6, fiber 1.2, carbs 3.8, protein 16.5

63. Chili Sea Bass

Preparation time: 30 minutes

Cooking time: 8 minutes

Servings: 1

Ingredients:

9 oz sea bass, trimmed

½ cup lemon juice

½ teaspoon salt

¼ teaspoon ground black pepper

1 Chile, chopped

6 teaspoons olive oil

1/3 cup water

1 yellow onion, sliced

Directions:

In the mixing bowl combine together lemon juice, olive oil, salt, ground black pepper Chile, and water.

Add onion and stir the liquid well.

After this, chop the sea bass roughly and place in the lemon mixture. Mix up gently and leave for 25 minutes to marinate.

After this, remove the fish from the marinade and transfer in the air fryer basket.

Spray it with oil spray and cook at 400F for 4 minutes from each side.

Nutrition: calories 317, fat 17.3, fiber 1.5, carbs 7.1, protein 31.3

64. Marinated Cod

Preparation time: 35 minutes

Cooking time: 15 minutes

Servings: 1

Ingredients:

13 oz cod fillet

1 tablespoon tomato paste

½ teaspoon ground coriander

½ teaspoon dried rosemary

½ teaspoon dried cilantro

4 tablespoons sunflower oil

½ teaspoon salt

1 tablespoon soy sauce, sugar-free

Directions:

In the mixing bowl combine together soy sauce and tomato paste.

Then add sunflower oil, cilantro, rosemary, coriander, and stir the mixture until homogenous and smooth.

After this, rub cod fillet with tomato sauce well and leave it for 30 minutes in the fridge to marinate.

Then wrap the fish in the foil and put in the air fryer.

Close the lid and cook it for 15 minutes at 375F.

Nutrition: calories 272, fat 19.8, fiber 0.4, carbs 1.6, protein 22.5

65. Glazed Pork Shoulder

Preparation Time: 15 minutes

Cooking Time: 18 minutes

Servings: 1

Ingredients:

1/3 cup soy sauce

2 pounds pork shoulder, cut into 1 1/2-inch thick slices

Directions:

In a bowl, put the soy sauce

Add the pork and generously coat it with marinade.

Cover and refrigerate to marinate for about 4–6 hours.

Set the temperature of the air fryer to 335°F. Grease an air fryer basket.

Place the pork shoulder into the prepared air fryer basket.

Air fry for about 10 minutes, and then another 6–8 minutes at 390°F.

Remove from the air fryer and transfer the pork shoulder onto a platter. With a piece of foil, cover the pork for about 10 minutes before serving. Enjoy!

Nutrition:

Calories: 475

Carbohydrate: 8 g

Protein: 36.1 g

Fat: 32.4 g

66.   Pork Shoulder with Pineapple Sauce

Preparation Time: 20 minutes

Cooking Time: 24 minutes

Servings: 1

Ingredients:

For Pork:

10 1/2 ounces pork shoulder, cut into bite-sized pieces

2 pinches Maggi seasoning

1 teaspoon light soy sauce

Dash sesame oil

1 egg

1/4 cup plain flour

For Sauce:

1 teaspoon olive oil

1 medium onion, sliced

1 tablespoon garlic, minced

1 large pineapple slice, cubed

1 medium tomato, chopped

2 tablespoons tomato sauce

2 tablespoons oyster sauce

1 tablespoon Worcestershire sauce

1 tablespoon water

1/2 tablespoon corn flour

Directions:

For the pork: In a large bowl, mix together the Maggi seasoning, soy sauce, and sesame oil.

Add the pork cubes and generously mix them with the mixture.

Refrigerate to marinate for about 4–6 hours.

In a shallow dish, beat the egg.

In another dish, place the plain flour.

Dip the cubed pork in a beaten egg, and then coat evenly with the flour.

Set the temperature of the air fryer to 248°F. Grease an air fryer basket.

Arrange pork cubes into the prepared air fryer basket in a single layer.

Air fry for about 20 minutes.

Meanwhile, for the sauce: in a skillet, heat oil over medium heat and sauté the onion and garlic for about 1 minute.

Add the pineapple, and tomato and cook for about 1 minute.

Add the tomato sauce, oyster sauce, Worcestershire sauce, and stir to combine.

Meanwhile, in a bowl, mix together the water and corn flour.

Add the corn flour mixture into the sauce, stirring continuously.

Cook until the sauce is thickened enough, stirring continuously.

Remove pork cubes from the air fryer and add them into the sauce.

Cook for about 1–2 minutes or until coated completely.

Remove from the heat and serve hot.

Nutrition:

Calories: 557

Carbohydrate: 57.5 g

Protein: 28.8 g

Fat: 25.1 g

67.   Air Fryer Ranch Pork Chops

Preparation Time: 15 minutes

Cooking Time: 10 minutes

Servings: 1

Ingredients:

2 tsb dry ranch salad dressing mix

4 boneless, center-cut pork chops, 1-inch thick

Cooking spray

Directions:

Grease pork chops with cooking spray.

Season both sides of the ribs with the ranch seasoning mixture and let stand for a few minutes.

Grease and preheat the fryer to 390 degrees F (200 degrees C).

Place the ribs in the fryer and cook for about 10 minutes. After the first 5 minutes, turn the ribs over.

Allow resting on a plate a few minutes before serving.

Nutrition:

Calories: 255

Fat: 8.4 g

Carbohydrates: 0.7 g

Protein: 41 g

68.   Rib-Eye Steak

Preparation Time: 2h and 10 minutes

Cooking Time: 15 minutes

Servings: 1

Ingredients:

2 tsb dry ranch salad dressing mix

4 boneless, center-cut pork chops, 1-inch thick

Cooking spray

Directions:

Marinate the steaks for more than 2 hours with the olive oil, soy sauce, and seasoning

Discard the marinade from the steaks and remove excess oil from the steaks.

Preheat the air fryer to 400 degrees F and cook the steaks for about 15 minutes. Turn them over halfway through cooking.

Allow resting for about 5 minutes before serving.

Nutrition:

Calories: 620

Fat: 40.3 g

Carbohydrates: 7.4 g

Protein: 45.1 g

69.   Breaded Air Fryer Pork Chops

Preparation Time: 10 minutes

Cooking Time: 10 minutes

Servings: 1

Ingredients:

1 teaspoon Cajun seasoning

1 ½ cups cheese and garlic croutons

2 eggs

4 boneless, center-cut pork chops

Cooking spray

Directions:

Preheat the air fryer to 390 degrees F.

Season the pork chops with Cajun seasoning.

Puree the croutons in a small food processor to a fine texture.

Beat the eggs in a bowl. Dip the ribs into the egg mixture first, then bread them.

Spray the air fryer basket with cooking spray and place the ribs inside. Cook for 10 minutes. Flip the ribs halfway through cooking.

Nutrition:

Calories: 230

Fat: 10.8 g

Carbohydrates: 9 g

Protein: 34 g

70. Glazed Pork Shoulder

Preparation Time: 15 minutes

Cooking Time: 18 minutes

Servings: 1

Ingredients:

1/3 cup soy sauce

2 pounds pork shoulder, cut into 1 1/2-inch thick slices

Directions:

In a bowl, put the soy sauce

Add the pork and generously coat it with marinade.

Cover and refrigerate to marinate for about 4–6 hours.

Set the temperature of the air fryer to 335°F. Grease an air fryer basket.

Place the pork shoulder into the prepared air fryer basket.

Air fry for about 10 minutes, and then another 6–8 minutes at 390°F.

Remove from the air fryer and transfer the pork shoulder onto a platter.

With a piece of foil, cover the pork for about 10 minutes before serving.

Enjoy!

Nutrition:

Calories: 475

Carbohydrate: 8 g

Protein: 36.1 g

Fat: 32.4 g

71. Pork Shoulder with Pineapple Sauce

Preparation Time: 20 minutes

Cooking Time: 24 minutes

Servings: 1

Ingredients:

For Pork:

10 1/2 ounces pork shoulder, cut into bite-sized pieces

2 pinches Maggi seasoning

1 teaspoon light soy sauce

Dash sesame oil

1 egg

1/4 cup plain flour

For Sauce:

1 teaspoon olive oil

1 medium onion, sliced

1 tablespoon garlic, minced

1 large pineapple slice, cubed

1 medium tomato, chopped

2 tablespoons tomato sauce

2 tablespoons oyster sauce

1 tablespoon Worcestershire sauce

1 tablespoon water

1/2 tablespoon corn flour

Directions:

For the pork: In a large bowl, mix together the Maggi seasoning, soy sauce, and sesame oil.

Add the pork cubes and generously mix them with the mixture.

Refrigerate to marinate for about 4–6 hours.

In a shallow dish, beat the egg.

In another dish, place the plain flour.

Dip the cubed pork in a beaten egg, and then coat evenly with the flour.

Set the temperature of the air fryer to 248°F. Grease an air fryer basket.

Arrange pork cubes into the prepared air fryer basket in a single layer.

Air fry for about 20 minutes.

Meanwhile, for the sauce: in a skillet, heat oil over medium heat and sauté the onion and garlic for about 1 minute.

Add the pineapple, and tomato and cook for about 1 minute.

Add the tomato sauce, oyster sauce, Worcestershire sauce, and stir to combine.

Meanwhile, in a bowl, mix together the water and corn flour.

Add the corn flour mixture into the sauce, stirring continuously.

Cook until the sauce is thickened enough, stirring continuously.

Remove pork cubes from the air fryer and add them into the sauce.

Cook for about 1-2 minutes or until coated completely.

Remove from the heat and serve hot.

Nutrition:

Calories: 557

Carbohydrate: 57.5 g

Protein: 28.8 g

Fat: 25.1 g

72. Rib-Eye Steak

Preparation Time: 2h and 10 minutes

Cooking Time: 15 minutes

Servings: 1

Ingredients:

2 tsb dry ranch salad dressing mix

4 boneless, center-cut pork chops, 1-inch thick

Cooking spray

Directions:

Marinate the steaks for more than 2 hours with the olive oil, soy sauce, and seasoning

Discard the marinade from the steaks and remove excess oil from the steaks.

Preheat the air fryer to 400 degrees F and cook the steaks for about 15 minutes. Turn them over halfway through cooking.

Allow resting for about 5 minutes before serving.

Nutrition:

Calories: 620

Fat: 40.3 g

Carbohydrates: 7.4 g

Protein: 45.1 g

73. Breaded Air Fryer Pork Chops

Preparation Time: 10 minutes

Cooking Time: 10 minutes

Servings: 1

Ingredients:

1 teaspoon Cajun seasoning

1 ½ cups cheese and garlic croutons

2 eggs

4 boneless, center-cut pork chops

Cooking spray

Directions:

Preheat the air fryer to 390 degrees F.

Season the pork chops with Cajun seasoning.

Puree the croutons in a small food processor to a fine texture.

Beat the eggs in a bowl. Dip the ribs into the egg mixture first, then bread them.

Spray the air fryer basket with cooking spray and place the ribs inside. Cook for 10 minutes. Flip the ribs halfway through cooking.

Nutrition:

Calories: 230

Fat: 10.8 g

Carbohydrates: 9 g

Protein: 34 g

74. Flank Steak Beef

Preparation Time: 10 minutes

Cooking Time: 20 minutes

Servings: 1

Ingredients:

1 pound flank steaks, sliced

¼ cup xanthum gum

2 teaspoon vegetable oil

½ teaspoon ginger

½ cup soy sauce

1 tablespoon garlic, minced

½ cup water

¾ cup swerve, packed

Directions:

Preheat the Air fryer to 390 o F and grease an Air fryer basket.

Coat the steaks with xanthum gum on both the sides and transfer into the Air fryer basket.

Cook for about 10 minutes and dish out in a platter.

Meanwhile, cook rest of the ingredients for the sauce in a saucepan.

Bring to a boil and pour over the steak slices to serve.

Nutrition: Calories: 372, Fat: 11.8g, Carbohydrates: 1.8g, Sugar: 27.3g, Protein: 34g, Sodium: 871mg

75. Pepper Pork Chops

Preparation Time: 15 minutes

Cooking Time: 6 minutes

Servings: 1

Ingredients:

2 pork chops

1 egg white

¾ cup xanthum gum

½ teaspoon sea salt

¼ teaspoon freshly ground black pepper

1 oil mister

Directions:

Preheat the Air fryer to 400 o F and grease an Air fryer basket.

Whisk egg white with salt and black pepper in a bowl and dip the pork chops in it.

Cover the bowl and marinate for about 20 minutes.

Pour the xanthum gum over both sides of the chops and spray with oil mister.

Arrange the chops in the Air fryer basket and cook for about 6 minutes.

Dish out in a bowl and serve warm.

Nutrition: Calories: 541, Fat: 34g, Carbohydrates: 3.4g, Sugar: 1g, Protein: 20.3g, Sodium: 547mg

76. Garlic Butter Pork Chops

Preparation Time: 10 minutes

Cooking Time: 8 minutes

Servings: 1

Ingredients:

4 pork chops

1 tablespoon coconut butter

2 teaspoons parsley

1 tablespoon coconut oil

2 teaspoons garlic, grated

Salt and black pepper, to taste

Directions:

Preheat the Air fryer to 350 o F and grease an Air fryer basket.

Mix all the seasonings, coconut oil, garlic, butter, and parsley in a bowl and coat the pork chops with it.

Cover the chops with foil and refrigerate to marinate for about 1 hour.

Remove the foil and arrange the chops in the Air fryer basket.

Cook for about 8 minutes and dish out in a bowl to serve warm.

Nutrition: Calories: 311, Fat: 25.5g, Carbohydrates: 1.4g, Sugar: 0.3g, Protein: 18.4g, Sodium: 58mg

77. Five Spice Pork

Preparation Time: 15 minutes

Cooking Time: 20 minutes

Servings: 1

Ingredients:

1-pound pork belly

2 tablespoons swerve

2 tablespoons dark soy sauce

1 tablespoon Shaoxing: cooking wine

2 teaspoons garlic, minced

2 teaspoons ginger, minced

1 tablespoon hoisin sauce

1 teaspoon Chinese Five Spice

Directions:

Preheat the Air fryer to 390 o F and grease an Air fryer basket.

Mix all the ingredients in a bowl and place in the Ziplock bag.

Seal the bag, shake it well and refrigerate to marinate for about 1 hour.

Remove the pork from the bag and arrange it in the Air fryer basket.

Cook for about 15 minutes and dish out in a bowl to serve warm.

Nutrition: Calories: 604, Fat: 30.6g, Carbohydrates: 1.4g, Sugar: 20.3g, Protein: 19.8g, Sodium: 834mg

78. Roasted Lamb

Preparation Time: 15 minutes

Cooking Time: 1 hour 30 minutes

Servings: 1

Ingredients:

2½ pounds half lamb leg roast, slits carved

2 garlic cloves, sliced into smaller slithers

1 tablespoon dried rosemary

1 tablespoon olive oil

Cracked Himalayan rock salt and cracked peppercorns, to taste

Directions:

Preheat the Air fryer to 400 o F and grease an Air fryer basket.

Insert the garlic slithers in the slits and brush with rosemary, oil, salt, and black pepper.

Arrange the lamb in the Air fryer basket and cook for about 15 minutes.

Set the Air fryer to 350 o F on the Roast mode and cook for 1 hour and 15 minutes.

Dish out the lamb chops and serve hot.

Nutrition: Calories: 246, Fat: 7.4g, Carbohydrates: 9.4g, Sugar: 6.5g, Protein: 37.2g, Sodium: 353mg

79. Juicy Pork Chops

Preparation Time: 10 minutes

Cooking Time: 16 minutes

Servings: 1

Ingredients:

4 pork chops, boneless

2 tsp. olive oil

½ tsp. celery seed

½ tsp. parsley

½ tsp. granulated onion

½ tsp. granulated garlic

¼ tsp. sugar

½ tsp. salt

Directions:

1. Add and mix together oil, celery seed, parsley, granulated onion, granulated garlic, sugar, and salt in a small bowl.

2. Rub seasoning mixture all over the pork chops.

3. Place pork chops on the air fryer oven pan and cook at 350 F for 8 minutes.

4. Turn pork chops to the other side and cook for 8 minutes more.

5. Serve and enjoy.

Nutrition:

Calories: 279 kcal

Fat: 22.3g

Carbs: 0.6g

Protein: 18.1g

CHAPTER 4: SNACKS AND DESSERTS

80.   Sugary Apple Fritters

Preparation Time: 10 minutes

Cooking Time: 10 minutes

Servings: 1

Ingredients:

2 red apples

1 teaspoon sugar

1 tablespoon flour

1 tablespoon semolina

1 teaspoon lemon juice

½ teaspoon ground cinnamon

1 teaspoon butter

1 egg

Directions:

1. Peel the apples and grate them.

2. Sprinkle the grated apples with the lemon juice.

3. Then add sugar, flour, semolina, and ground cinnamon.

4. Mix the mixture and crack the egg.

5. Mix the apple mixture carefully.

6. Preheat the air fryer to 370 F.

7. Toss the butter in the air fryer basket and melt it.

8. When the butter is melted – make the medium fritters from the apple mixture. Use 2 spoons for this step.

9. Place the fritters in the air fryer basket and cook for 6 minutes.

10. After this, flip the fritters to another side and cook for 2 minutes more.

11. Dry the cooked fritters with the help of the paper towel and serve.

Nutrition:

Calories: 207 kcal

Fat: 4.6g

Carbs: 40.3g

Protein: 4.5g

81. Baked Bacon Potatoes

Preparation Time: 5 minutes

Cooking Time: 10 minutes

Servings: 1

Ingredients:

¼ cup chopped scallions

1 cup grated cheddar cheese

3 russet potatoes, cleaned and cut into 1-inch rounds

¼ cup butter

3 tablespoon bacon bits, cooked and crumbled

Directions:

1. Grease a baking pan with some cooking spray. Place potato over the pan; brush with butter and top with scallions and cheese.

2. Place Instant Vortex over the kitchen platform. Arrange to drip pan in the lower position. Press "Bake," set timer to 15 minutes, and set the temperature to 400°F. Instant Vortex will start pre-heating.

3. When Instant Vortex is pre-heated, it will display "Add Food" on its screen. Open the door, and take out the middle roasting tray.

4. Place the pan over the tray and push it back; close door and cooking will start. Midway, it will display "Turn Food" on its screen; ignore it, and it will continue to cook after 10 seconds. Cook until cheese is bubbly.

5. Open the door after the cooking cycle is over; serve warm with bacon on top.

Nutrition:

Calories: 330 kcal

Fat: 12g

Carbs: 48g

Protein: 7.5g

82. Raspberry Cream Roll-Ups

Preparation Time:

Cooking Time:

Servings: 1

Ingredients:

1 cup of fresh raspberries, rinsed and patted dry

½ cup of cream cheese, softened to room temperature

¼ cup of brown sugar

¼ cup of sweetened condensed milk

1 egg

1 teaspoon of corn starch

spring roll wrappers (any brand will do, we like Blue Dragon or Tasty Joy, both available through Target or Walmart, or any large grocery chain)

¼ cup of water

Directions:

1 Cover the basket of the air fryer oven with a lining of tin foil, leaving the edges uncovered to allow air to circulate through the basket. Preheat the air fryer oven to 350 degrees.

2 In a mixing bowl, combine the cream cheese, brown sugar, condensed milk, cornstarch, and egg. Beat or whip thoroughly, until all ingredients are completely mixed and fluffy, thick and stiff.

3 Spoon even amounts of the creamy filling into each spring roll wrapper, then top each dollop of filling with several raspberries.

4 Roll up the wraps around the creamy raspberry filling, and seal the seams with a few dabs of water.

5 Place each roll on the foil-lined air fryer basket, seams facing down.

6 Set the air fryer oven timer to 10 minutes during cooking; shake the handle of the fryer basket to ensure a nice even surface crisp.

7 After 10 minutes, when the air fryer oven shuts off, the spring rolls should be golden brown and perfect on the outside, while the raspberries and cream filling will have cooked together in a glorious fusion. Remove with tongs and serve hot or cold.

Nutrition:

Calories: 351 kcal

Fat: 20.1g

Protein: 4.3g

Sugar: 5.6g

83. Apricots in Blankets

Preparation Time: 20 minutes

Cooking Time: 24 minutes

Servings: 1

Ingredients:

dried apricots, halved lengthwise

2 ounces cream cheese

½ sheet frozen puff pastry, thawed

1 tablespoons honey mustard

1 tablespoons butter, melted

Directions:

1 Stuff each apricot half with a teaspoon of cream cheese and set aside.

2 Roll out the puff pastry until it is 6 by 12 inches. Cut in half lengthwise for two 3-by-12-inch rectangles. Cut each rectangle into six 3-inch strips for a total of 12 puff pastry strips.

3 Spread 1 teaspoon of honey mustard onto each strip. Place a filled apricot on each strip and roll up the pastry, pinching the seam closed but leaving the ends open.

4 Place 6 filled pastries in the air fryer basket. Brush the top of each with some of the melted butter.

5 Set or preheat the air fryer to 375°F. Put the basket in the air fryer. Air fry until the pastry is golden brown for 8 to 12 minutes. Repeat with the other six pastries, then serve.

Nutrition:

Calories: 137 kcal

Protein: 2g

Fat: 9g

Carbs: 12g

84. Radish Chips

Preparation Time: 20 minutes

Cooking Time: 18 minutes

Servings: 1

Ingredients:

large radishes

1 tablespoon olive oil

½ teaspoon sea salt

1 teaspoon curry powder

Directions:

1 Scrub the radishes and trim off the stem and root ends.

2 Using a sharp knife, slice the radishes into thin rounds, about ⅛ inch thick. Pat the radish slices dry with a paper towel.

3 Put the radishes into the air fryer basket and drizzle with the oil; toss to coat. Sprinkle with the salt and toss again.

4 Set or preheat the air fryer to 400°F. Set the basket in the air fryer and fry for 14 to 18 minutes, tossing once during cooking time, until the radish chips are crisp and light golden brown. Remove the basket; sprinkle the chips with the curry powder and toss.

5 Serve immediately or let cool and store in an airtight container at room temperature for up to 3 days.

Nutrition:

Calories: 17 kcal

Protein: 0g

Fat: 2g

Carbs: 1g

85. Air Fried Corn

Preparation Time: 5 minutes

Cooking Time: 10 minutes

Servings: 1

Ingredients:

1 cup corn kernels

2½ tablespoons butter

Directions:

In a saucepan that fits your air fryer, mix the corn with the butter.

Place the pan inside the air fryer and cook at 400 degrees F for 10 minutes.

Serve as a snack and enjoy!

Nutrition:

Calories: 70 kcal

Fat: 2g

Fiber: 2g

Carbs: 7g

Protein: 3g

86. Avocado and Raspberries Cake

Preparation Time: 40 minutes

Cooking Time: 15 minutes

Servings: 1

Ingredients:

2 avocados, peeled, pitted and mashed

4 oz. raspberries

1 cup swerve

1 cup almonds flour

4 eggs, whisked

4 tbsp. butter; melted

3 tsp. baking powder

Directions:

Take a bowl and mix all the ingredients, toss, pour this into a cake pan that fits the air fryer after you've lined it with parchment paper.

Put the pan in the fryer and cook at 340°F for 30 minutes

Leave the cake to cool down, slice and serve.

Nutrition: Calories: 193; Fat: 4g; Fiber: 2g; Carbs: 5g; Protein: 5g

87. Walnut and Vanilla Bars

Preparation Time: 21 minutes

Cooking Time: 10 minutes

Servings: 1

Ingredients:

1 egg

¼ cup almond flour

¼ cup walnuts; chopped.

1/3 cup cocoa powder

7 tbsp. ghee; melted

3 tbsp. swerve

½ tsp. baking soda

1 tsp. vanilla extract

Directions:

Take a bowl and mix all the ingredients and stir well.

Spread this on a baking sheet that fits your air fryer lined with parchment paper.

Put it in the fryer and cook at 330°F and bake for 16 minutes

Leave the bars to cool down, cut and serve

Nutrition: Calories: 182; Fat: 12g; Fiber: 1g; Carbs: 3g; Protein: 6g

88. Plum Cream

Preparation Time: 25 minutes

Cooking Time: 10 minutes

Servings: 1

Ingredients:

1 lb. plums, pitted and chopped.

1 ½ cups heavy cream

¼ cup swerve

1 tbsp. lemon juice

Directions:

Take a bowl and mix all the ingredients and whisk really well.

Divide this into 4 ramekins, put them in the air fryer and cook at 340°F for 20 minutes. Serve cold

Nutrition: Calories: 171; Fat: 4g; Fiber: 2g; Carbs: 4g; Protein: 4g

89.   Mini Lava Cakes

Preparation Time: 30 minutes

Cooking Time: 10 minutes

Servings: 1

Ingredients:

3 oz. dark chocolate; melted

2 eggs, whisked

¼ cup coconut oil; melted

1 tbsp. almond flour

2 tbsp. swerve

¼ tsp. vanilla extract

Cooking spray

Directions:

In bowl, combine all the ingredients except the cooking spray and whisk really well.

Divide this into 4 ramekins greased with cooking spray, put them in the fryer and cook at 360°F for 20 minutes

Nutrition: Calories: 161; Fat: 12g; Fiber: 1g; Carbs: 4g; Protein: 7g

90. Lemon Blackberries Cake

Preparation Time: 35 minutes

Cooking Time: 10 minutes

Servings: 1

Ingredients:

2 eggs, whisked

¼ cup almond milk

1 ½ cups almond flour

1 cup blackberries; chopped.

2 tbsp. ghee; melted

4 tbsp. swerve

1 tsp. lemon zest, grated

1 tsp. lemon juice

½ tsp. baking powder

Directions:

Take a bowl and mix all the ingredients and whisk well.

Pour this into a cake pan that fits the air fryer lined with parchment paper, put the pan in your air fryer and cook at 340°F for 25 minutes. Cool the cake down, slice and serve

Nutrition: Calories: 193; Fat: 5g; Fiber: 1g; Carbs: 4g; Protein: 4g

91. Chocolate Mug Cake

Preparation Time: 15 minutes

Cooking Time: 13 minutes

Servings: 1

Ingredients:

¼ cup self-rising flour

1 tablespoon cocoa powder

3 tablespoons whole milk

5 tablespoons caster sugar

3 tablespoons coconut oil

Directions:

Preheat the Air fryer to 390 o F and grease a large mug lightly.

Mix all the ingredients in a shallow mug until well combined.

Arrange the mug into the Air fryer basket and cook for about 13 minutes.

Dish out and serve warm.

Nutrition: Calories: 729, Fat: 43.3g, Carbohydrates: 88.8g, Sugar: 62.2g, Protein: 5.7g, Sodium: 20mg

92. Dark Chocolate Cheesecake

Preparation Time: 20 minutes

Cooking Time: 34 minutes

Servings: 1

Ingredients:

3 eggs, whites and yolks separated

1 cup dark chocolate, chopped

½ cup cream cheese, softened

2 tablespoons cocoa powder

¼ cup dates jam

2 tablespoons powdered sugar

Directions:

Preheat the Air fryer to 285 o F and grease a cake pan lightly.

Refrigerate egg whites in a bowl to chill before using.

Microwave chocolate and cream cheese on high for about 3 minutes.

Remove from microwave and whisk in the egg yolks.

Whisk together egg whites until firm peaks form and combine with the chocolate mixture.

Transfer the mixture into a cake pan and arrange in the Air fryer basket.

Cook for about 30 minutes and dish out.

Dust with powdered sugar and spread dates jam on top to serve.

Nutrition: Calories: 298, Fat: 18.3g, Carbohydrates: 29.7g, Sugar: 24.5g, Protein: 6.3g, Sodium: 119mg

93. Cream Doughnuts

Preparation Time: 15 minutes

Cooking Time: 16 minutes

Servings: 1

Ingredients:

4 tablespoons butter, softened and divided

2 egg yolks

2¼ cups plain flour

1½ teaspoons baking powder

½ cup sugar

1 teaspoon salt

½ cup sour cream

½ cup heavy cream

Directions:

Preheat the Air fryer to 355 o F and grease an Air fryer basket lightly.

Sift together flour, baking powder and salt in a large bowl.

Add sugar and cold butter and mix until a coarse crumb is formed.

Stir in the egg yolks, ½ of the sour cream and 1/3 of the flour mixture and mix until a dough is formed.

Add remaining sour cream and 1/3 of the flour mixture and mix until well combined.

Stir in the remaining flour mixture and combine well.

Roll the dough into ½ inch thickness onto a floured surface and cut into donuts with a donut cutter.

Coat butter on both sides of the donuts and arrange in the Air fryer basket.

Cook for about 8 minutes until golden and top with heavy cream to serve.

Nutrition: Calories: 297, Fats: 13g, Carbohydrates: 40.7g, Sugar: 12.6g, Proteins: 5g, Sodium: 346mg

94. Coconut Balls

Preparation time: 10 minutes

Cooking time: 40 minutes

Servings: 1

Ingredients:

1 egg white

4 tablespoons coconut flakes

2 tablespoons Erythritol

Directions:

Mix up together egg white and Erythritol and whisk the mixture till you get the strong peaks
After this, slowly add coconut flakes and stir the mixture.
Line the air fryer basket with baking paper.
With the help of the spoon make "clouds" and place them in the air fryer or make them directly in the air fryer.
Cook the coconut clouds for 40 minutes at 330F or until the "clouds" are light brown.
Nutrition: calories 44, fat 1.7, fiber 0.5, carbs 6.8, protein 1.1

95. Jicama Fries

Preparation Time: 30 minutes

Cooking Time: 12 minutes

Servings: 1

Ingredients:

1 small jicama; peeled.

¼ tsp. onion powder.

¾ tsp. chili powder

¼ tsp. ground black pepper

¼ tsp. garlic powder.

Directions:

Cut jicama into matchstick-sized pieces.

Place pieces into a small bowl and sprinkle with remaining ingredients. Place the fries into the air fryer basket

Adjust the temperature to 350 Degrees F and set the timer for 20 minutes. Toss the basket two or three times during cooking. Serve warm.

Nutrition: Calories: 37; Protein: 0.8g; Fiber: 4.7g; Fat: 0.1g; Carbs: 8.7g

96. Kale Chips

Preparation Time: 10 minutes

Cooking Time: 20 minutes

Servings: 1

Ingredients:

4 cups stemmed kale

½ tsp. salt

2 tsp. avocado oil

Directions:

Take a large bowl, toss kale in avocado oil and sprinkle with salt. Place into the air fryer basket.

Adjust the temperature to 400 Degrees F and set the timer for 5 minutes. Kale will be crispy when done. Serve immediately.

Nutrition: Calories: 25; Protein: 0.5g; Fiber: 0.4g; Fat: 2.2g; Carbs: 1.1g

97. Finger Cookies

Preparation time: 15 minutes

Cooking time: 8 minutes

Servings: 1

Ingredients:

1 cup almond flour

¼ cup coconut cream

1 egg, beaten

1 teaspoon vanilla extract

3 tablespoon Erythritol

2 oz walnuts, chopped

1 teaspoon poppy seeds

1 teaspoon baking powder

½ teaspoon lemon zest, grated

1 tablespoon almond butter

Directions:

In the mixing bowl combine all ingredients and knead the soft dough with the help of the fingertips.

After this, cut the dough into 6 pieces and roll the shape of "fingers" from every piece.

Line the air fryer basket with baking paper and arrange the finger cookies inside.

Cook the cookies for 8 minutes at 365F. Flip the cookies on another side after 4 minutes of cooking.

Nutrition: calories 204, fat 10.2, fiber 1.6, carbs 22.8, protein 6.3

98. Spicy Air-Fryer Sunflower Seeds

Preparation time: 10 minutes

Cooking Time: 10 minutes

Servings: 1

2 cups unsalted sunflower seeds

2 teaspoons olive oil

2 teaspoons chili garlic paste

¼ teaspoon salt

1 teaspoon granular erythritol

Directions:

1. Preheat air fryer at 325°F/ 160°C for 3 minutes. 2. Combine all ingredients in a medium bowl until seeds are well coated. 3. Place seeds in ungreased air fryer basket cooking for 5 minutes, and shake basket cooking for an additional 5 minutes. 4. Transfer it to a medium serving bowl and serve it.

Nutrition: Calories 815; Fat 73.15g; Sodium 169mg; Carbs 30.37g; Fiber 7.3g; Sugar 13.51g; Protein 22.53g

99. Roasted Jack-O'-Lantern Seeds with black pepper

Preparation time: 10 minutes

Cooking Time: 13 minutes

Servings: 1

2 cups fresh pumpkin seeds

1 tablespoon butter, melted

1 teaspoon salt, divided

½ teaspoon onion powder

½ teaspoon dried parsley

½ teaspoon garlic powder

½ teaspoon dried dill

¼ teaspoon dried chives

¼ teaspoon dry mustard

¼ teaspoon celery seed

¼ teaspoon freshly ground black pepper

Directions:

1. Preheat air fryer at 325°F/ 160°C for 3 minutes. 2. Toss seeds with butter and ½ teaspoon salt in a medium bowl. 3. Place seed mixture in ungreased air fryer basket cooking for 7 minutes. 4. Use a spatula turning seeds, and then cook for an additional 6 minutes. 5. Transfer it to a medium serving bowl, and toss it with remaining ingredients. 6. Serve it.

Nutrition: Calories 368; Fat 31.91g; Sodium 760mg; Carbs 9.44g; Fiber 4g; Sugar 0.8g; Protein 17.82g

100. Tasty Ranch Roasted Almonds

Preparation time: 5 minutes

Cooking Time: 6 minutes

Servings: 1

2 cups raw almonds

2 tablespoons unsalted butter, melted

½ (1-ounce) ranch dressing mix packet

Directions:

1. Toss almonds in butter to evenly coat in a large bowl. 2. Sprinkle ranch mix over almonds and toss them. 3. Place almonds into the air fryer basket. 4. Adjust the temperature to 320°F/ 160°C and set the timer for 6 minutes. 5. Shake the basket two or three times during cooking. 6. Cool it at least 20 minutes. 7. Store it in an airtight container up to 3 days.

Nutrition: Calories 19; Fat 2.08g; Sodium 1mg; Carbs 0.06g; Fiber 0g; Sugar 0.01g; Protein 0.18g

101. Air-Fryer Jalapeño Poppers

Preparation time: 10 minutes

Cooking Time: 18 minutes

Servings: 1

1 tablespoon olive oil

¼ pound ground pork

2 tablespoons pitted and finely diced Kalamata olives

2 tablespoons feta cheese

1 ounce cream cheese, room temperature

½ teaspoon dried mint leaves

6 large jalapeños, sliced in half lengthwise and seeded

Directions:

1. Heat olive oil over medium-high heat 30 seconds in a medium skillet. 2. Add pork and cook it for 6 minutes until it is no longer pink. Drain fat. 3. Preheat air fryer to 350°F/ 175°C for 3 minutes. 4. Combine cooked pork, olives, feta cheese, cream cheese, and mint leaves in a medium bowl. 5. Press pork mixture into peppers. 6. Place half of poppers in ungreased air fryer basket for 6 minutes. 7. Transfer it to a medium serving plate and repeat cooking with remaining poppers. 8. Serve it warm.

Nutrition: Calories 108; Fat 8.91g; Sodium 138mg; Carbs 0.78g; Fiber 0.1g; Sugar 0.54g; Protein 6.05g

102. Simple Baked Brie with Orange Marmalade and Spiced Walnuts

Preparation time: 10 minutes

Cooking Time: 22 minutes

Servings: 1

1 cup walnuts

1 large egg white, beaten

⅛ teaspoon ground cumin

⅛ teaspoon cayenne pepper

1 teaspoon ground cinnamon

¼ teaspoon powdered erythritol

1 (8-ounce) round Brie

2 tablespoons sugar-free orange marmalade

Directions:

1. Preheat air fryer at 325°F/ 160°C for 3 minutes. 2. Combine walnuts with egg white in a small bowl, and set aside. 3. Combine cumin, cayenne pepper, cinnamon, and erythritol in a separate small bowl, adding walnuts, drained of excess egg white, and toss them. 4. Place walnuts in ungreased air fryer basket cooking for 6 minutes, and then toss nuts cooking for an additional 6 minutes. 5. Transfer them to a small bowl and cool it about 5 minutes until it's easy to handle. After it's cooled, chop it into smaller bits. 6. Adjust air fryer temperature to 400°F/ 200°C, and put Brie in an ungreased pizza pan or on a piece of parchment paper cut to size of air fryer basket cook for 10 minutes. 7. Transfer Brie to a medium serving plate and garnish it with orange marmalade and spiced walnuts.

Nutrition: Calories 661; Fat 55.97g; Sodium 1083mg; Carbs 3.03g; Fiber 1.1g; Sugar 1.17g; Protein 38.07g

103. Crusted Pickle Chips

Preparation time: 1 hour 20 minutes

Cooking time: 12 minutes

Servings: 1

Oil, for spraying

2 cups sliced dill or sweet pickles, drained

1 cup buttermilk

2 cups all-purpose flour

2 large eggs, beaten

2 cups panko bread crumbs

¼ teaspoon salt

Directions:

1. Prepare the air fryer basket by lining it with parchment and spray lightly with oil. 2. In a shallow bowl, combine the pickles and buttermilk and let soak for at least 1 hour, then drain. 3. Place the bread crumbs, flour, and beaten eggs in separate bowls. 4. Coat each pickle chip lightly in the flour, dip in the eggs, and dredge in the bread crumbs. Be sure each one is evenly coated. 5. Place the pickle chips in the prepared basket, sprinkle with the salt, and spray lightly with oil. Work in batches as needed. 6. Cook at 390°F/ 200°C for 5 minutes, flip, and cook for another 5 to 7 minutes, or until crispy. Serve hot.

Nutrition: Calories 335; Fat 4.2g; Sodium 980mg; Carbs 61.5g; Fiber 3g; Sugar 5g; Protein 11.8g

104. Spicy Cumin Chickpeas

Preparation time: 5 minutes

Cooking time: 17 minutes

Servings: 1

Oil, for spraying

1 (15½-ounce) can chickpeas, drained

1 teaspoon chili powder

½ teaspoon ground cumin

½ teaspoon salt

½ teaspoon granulated garlic

2 teaspoons lime juice

Directions:

1. Prepare the air fryer basket by lining it with parchment and spray lightly with oil. Place the chickpeas in the prepared basket. 2. Cook at 390°F/ 200°C for 17 minutes, shaking or stirring the chickpeas and spraying lightly with oil every 5 to 7 minutes. 3. Mix the chili powder, garlic, cumin, and salt in a small bowl. 4. When there is 2 to 3 minutes remained, sprinkle half of the seasoning mix over the chickpeas. Finish cooking. 5. Place the chickpeas to a medium bowl and toss with the remaining seasoning mix and the lime juice. Serve immediately.

Nutrition: Calories 209; Fat 4.3g; Sodium 774mg; Carbs 34g; Fiber 9.7g; Sugar 6g; Protein 10.6g

105. Apple Doughnuts

Preparation Time: 20 minutes

Cooking Time: 5 minutes

Servings: 1

Ingredients:

2½ cups plus 2 tablespoons all-purpose flour

1½ teaspoons baking powder

2 tablespoons unsalted butter, softened

1 egg

½ pink lady apple, peeled, cored and grated

1 cup apple cider

½ teaspoon ground cinnamon

½ teaspoon salt

½ cup brown sugar

Directions:

Preheat the Air fryer to 360 o F and grease an Air fryer basket lightly.

Boil apple cider in a medium pan over medium-high heat and reduce the heat.

Let it simmer for about 15 minutes and dish out in a bowl.

Sift together flour, baking powder, baking soda, cinnamon, and salt in a large bowl.

Mix the brown sugar, egg, cooled apple cider and butter in another bowl.

Stir in the flour mixture and grated apple and mix to form a dough.

Wrap the dough with a plastic wrap and refrigerate for about 30 minutes.

Roll the dough into 1-inch thickness and cut the doughnuts with a doughnut cutter.

Arrange the doughnuts into the Air fryer basket and cook for about 5 minutes, flipping once in between.

Dish out and serve warm.

Nutrition: Calories: 433, Fat: 11g, Carbohydrates: 78.3g, Sugar: 35g, Protein: 6.8g, Sodium: 383mg

CONCLUSION

Thank you for reading this cookbook. An Air Fryer is a magically transformed kitchen appliance that allows you to fry with little or no oil at all. This type of product employs Rapid Air technology, which provides a new way to fry with less oil. This new invention cooks food by circulating superheated air and produces 80% low-fat food. Although the food is fried with less oil, you should not be concerned because the food produced by the Air Fryer tastes the same as that produced by the deep-frying method.

Air fryers allow you to enjoy fried foods guilt-free and in a healthy way. It circulates extremely hot air containing minuscule oil droplets from your food, resulting in a soft interior and crisp and crunchy exterior. In the presence of hot air, an air fryer causes a reaction between the sugars and amino acids in your food, resulting in enhanced flavor and color.

An Air Fryer ensures that the food is completely cooked. The exhaust fan located at the top of the cooking chamber assists the food in quickly reaching the same heating temperature in all parts, resulting in the best and healthiest cooked food. Furthermore, cooking with an Air Fryer is beneficial for those who are pressed for time. For example, an Air Fryer requires only half a teaspoon of oil and 10 minutes to prepare a medium bowl of crispy French fries.

Aside from serving healthier food, an Air Fryer has a few other advantages. Because an Air Fryer allows you to cook with less or no oil for certain foods, it automatically reduces the fat and cholesterol content of the food. No one will refuse to eat fried food because they are concerned about the greasy and fat content. Having fried food without feeling guilty is a form of indulging your tongue. Aside from having low fat and cholesterol, consuming oil sparingly saves money that can be used for other purposes. Your food can also be reheated using an Air Fryer. When you reheat fried leftovers, it will usually serve reheated greasy food with some addition of unhealthy reuse oil. This process undoubtedly increases the saturated fat content of fried foods. An Air Fryer allows you to reheat food without worrying about extra oils that the food may absorb.

It is a sophisticated multi-purpose appliance because it can roast chicken, make steak, grill fish, and even bake a cake. An Air Fryer, with its built-in air filter, filters the air and protects your kitchen from smoke and grease.

The use of an air fryer reduces the need for oil, thereby reducing calories and bad cholesterol. Furthermore, it improves the food's quality. Everything is prepared right in front of your eyes. Preservatives and excessive spices and salt are not permitted in the recipes. You get the best of both worlds.

It comes as no surprise that using an air fryer for healthy living is a good idea. You can still eat your favorite fried foods with fewer calories and more added flavors while also leading a healthy, balanced life and lowering your risk of Obesity, Diabetes, and other diseases. An air fryer is a simple and innovative way to cook. Grab it quickly and say hello to a clean and healthy kitchen.

Good luck.

Printed in Great Britain
by Amazon